CURATING NEW MEDIA
THIRD BALTIC INTERNATIONAL SEMINAR
10–12 MAY 2001

Also available in the B.READ series:

Curating New Media

Third BALTIC International Seminar
10–12 May 2001

Tamas Banovich
Vuk Cosic
Matthew Gansallo
Karen Guthrie and Nina Pope
Iliyana Nedkova
Julian Stallabrass
Thomson & Craighead
Mark Tribe

Edited by Sarah Cook, Beryl Graham & Sarah Martin

First published in 2002 by BALTIC.

BALTIC
P.O.Box 158
Gateshead NE8 1FG
Great Britain
www.balticmill.com

© BALTIC, CRUMB, University of Sunderland and the authors

ISBN 1-903655-06-4

Design by Ripe Design, The New Inn, Bridge Street, Blaydon-on-Tyne.
Printed and bound in Great Britain by Cox and Wyman Ltd.
Cardiff Road, Reading, Berkshire.

Distributed by Cornerhouse Publications Ltd., 70 Oxford Street, Manchester M1 5NH.

Curating New Media

CONTENTS

EDITOR'S NOTES ON THE STRUCTURE
OF THIS BOOK

The seminar Curating New Media, jointly organised by
BALTIC and the Curatorial Resource for Upstart Media
Bliss (CRUMB) aimed to provide a forum for curators,
producers, organisers, funders and artists working with
new media to discuss issues ranging from techniques of
presentation to remote networking. The discussions on the
first day addressed the tensions between Net-based
practice and the art world, particularly the museum,
inspired by the invited presence of net.artist Vuk Cosic
(who created BALTIC's first Web-based commission in
January 2000, thisistherealmatrix.com). The second day's
presentations addressed artistic practice in non-institu-
tional (and non-physical) spaces – artist/curator hybrids
spoke about building their own media-based production
models which ranged from project management across
borders to self-commissioning partnerships.

The seminar was structured to allow for a great deal of
discussion between the speakers and attendees – on the
first day large chunks of time were deemed 'open forums'

in recognition of the expertise of the conference participants. For the sake of clarity, in this publication we have
compiled these open forums into one section that appears
at the end of day one.

As is the case with any publication disseminating the
results of a seminar or conference event, consideration
has to be given to the visual material presented alongside
the talks. The presenters spoke about art, interactive
installations, one-day events, exhibitions and archival
resources, and as documentation they showed Websites,
videos, DVDs and old-fashioned slides. In honour of Julian
Stallabrass – who always shows slides of screengrabs
from Websites rather than the real Websites themselves
for the accelerated nostalgia such a vision induces – we
have inserted [Slide] in the text as a generic marker
indicating accompanying visual (and often online) material.
At the end of the book we have included a list of URLs for
further reference. Also, as the language of new media
becomes vernacular we have tried to be consistent in our
editing but have allowed for idiosyncracies: for instance, to
describe art on the Internet Julian Stallabrass says 'Net
Art', Mark Tribe says 'net-art' and Vuk Cosic says 'net.art'
(a term he coined to describe the group of artists of which
he was a part). Rather than standardise them, we've left
these as they are.

For all the other missing links I invite you to seek out
CRUMB's CD-ROM (released December 2001), which
includes documentation (including images and hyperlinks)
from the seminar. On both the CD-ROM and the CRUMB
Website you can find abridged versions of all of the talks,
as well as the full text of both my and Vuk Cosic's introduction and the Artists' Roundtable which, for the sake of
space, don't appear in this book.

A number of free, public art events in Newcastle,
Gateshead and Sunderland were scheduled to coincide
with the seminar. BALTIC invited Kate Rich to bring her
'Small Radius Cinema' programme of short digital and

Web-based films from its usual home in Middlesborough to Newcastle. The schedule of what Kate screened in the ethereal top-floor lounge of the Quality Hotel is included here.

Lastly, this seminar would not have been possible without the unflagging support of Beryl Graham at the University of Sunderland and BALTIC curator Vicki Lewis and her team. Thanks are especially due to Dave Pipkin, John Smith and Tom Cullen for flawlessly creating and executing the seminar infrastructure, technology and audio documentation. Emma Thomas, Hannah Barnes and Sophie Thomson managed the microphones during the discussions and Sarah Martin has helped greatly in producing this publication. My heartfelt appreciation to you all. This book is dedicated to Vuk Cosic.

Sarah Cook

INTRODUCTION: SUNE NORDGREN, SARAH COOK AND VUK COSIC

SUNE NORDGREN:

I'm Sune Nordgren, director of BALTIC. First of all, a very warm welcome to all of you, to this three-day seminar at St. Mary's Church which is our base during the pre-opening period. It's a Visitor Centre for the Gateshead Quays development as well as the offices for BALTIC and the new Music Centre here in Gateshead.

This seminar – called 'Curating New Media' – is the third in the series of International Seminars organised by BALTIC during the pre-opening period, which has been about three years now. I arrived here in early 1998 and we've been working on this project ever since: there are thirteen people in the BALTIC team at the moment. The seminars have been very important for us because they give us great feedback. We are doing something that we believe is completely new and unique. So the seminars give us feedback and confidence from professionals and colleagues around the world that we are on the right track with this project.

The first seminar was called 'New Sites – New Art' and posed the question, 'Can you create an institution today that is not really an institution, but is a very open-minded place, not only reflecting on the art of our time, but also creating it and being a creative partner in it?' That seminar gave us lots of ideas to continue this work. The second one was called 'Artists at Work' and was completely focused on commissioning artists and the Artist-in-Residence programme, which will be a very important part of BALTIC's activities and will see artists, writers, publishers and curators invited to BALTIC to work with us.

So this is the third seminar and I think it is very important for us. We know that new media will be an important part of the BALTIC programme. We will try to accommodate all kinds of work, because even if we spend lots of money on a cutting-edge new media lab at BALTIC, there will still be artists who want to use 16 mm film, for example. So we will try to be as flexible as possible and also work with institutions and organisations around the region.

So, thank you very much for coming here and I hope that you will enjoy your stay in Gateshead. Now I'll hand over to Sarah.

SARAH COOK:

Thank you Sune. [...]
We are going to start off by framing briefly the questions: why this seminar, why this topic and why these people to come and talk about this topic?

I think between us Vuk and I have been to a number of different seminars and conferences concerning new media and particularly curating, and they have varied enormously – from workshops where producers and scientists are brought together and work very intensively in a laboratory environment, to sitting in Trieste eating ice cream for three days and then at the end speaking to the public about what you've learnt. This is a more formal setting but I think that it will be useful to be able to look at case studies in an in-depth way and listen to people speak to their experience.

The first questions I have concern the practicalities of how curators deal with media and technology – how the work is getting made, how it is getting shown, how it is getting distributed and how it is out in the world. There is a great need, as far as institutions are concerned, to look at the issue of installation and consider the questions that arise when you put a computer in a gallery. I have put together some images of various projects to address this. [Slides] [...]

Vuk Cosic is here because we've recently commissioned a project from him – 'thisistherealmatrix.com'. We had a computer in this church as a way of giving people an interface to the site and also provided a telephone – if you've seen the film 'The Matrix', then you'll know how important they are – so you could pick it up and speak directly to Vuk. Vuk's had a lot of experience in having his work shown in various settings and now it is going to be at the Venice Biennale and that opens up a whole new can of worms. I think it is great to have him here as a kind of provocation to these questions and I hope that he participates in that way too and sticks his two cents in.

VUK COSIC:

Hi there. [...] I guess that the reason I'm here really is because of a number of talks I gave that Sarah saw. And all the time I complain about curators – so it serves me right, here I am! I always thought of how I used to do net.art and then I stopped because there was a lot of pressure from the art world to do shows all the time and to be in some histories and essays – and we only wanted to do art. Now this thing is interfering with our noble aspirations and so on. I had to switch: I moved elsewhere and I'm doing other things. Art is much more about technology. And then when they ask me, 'how come you had to switch?' I usually say a sentence that I will now repeat and if you wish, I will repeat again later; I think it makes sense. I somehow tend to insist that, at least in my experiences – now here comes the sentence – 'curatorial decisions are usually made in such a way that they are there to justify the hardware investment and are not the reflection of any understanding.' Now this may be a rude thing to say, especially in a room full of curators of new media art! But you must understand me. Sometimes I feel like – now don't take this the wrong way – but I feel like, let's say, a lesbian, Jewish, handicapped... what else... I don't know... person. But someone that somehow fits the bill or shows up in your political correctness Excel table in four columns at the same time. So I look good in statistics and I'm now sorry that I've never explored this systemati-cally and that I've never really done a user survey – well a curator survey – where I would have a questionnaire and have all these people answer questions. One of them would be, 'what on earth are you seeing in what you are showing here of mine?'

I spoke over a perfectly good English breakfast with Julian Stallabrass about segregation – is that the word we used? There have been shows where you could see artists belonging to these two otherwise separate galaxies of old and new media, let's say. I've been to shows with some pretty famous people in some grand-slam galleries, but the format was always such that we never met, or at least if we did meet, it was never the fruit of any curator's intention. It was only an accidental invite that you happened to get to come to some gala dinner inside the Stedjelik or a standing party inside some embassy and there you might possibly, if you had Vaseline on your elbows, come across some accomplished artists who you would spend twenty minutes with. That was always a surprise for me because in my world of net.art, the basic condition was that we are in touch and then we would possibly decide not to talk. But here the basic condition is completely the opposite. It is like we absolutely shut up. I don't tell you anything and you don't tell me anything, and maybe we just might exchange a tiny little bit and I might give you a name of a curator or a name of a restaurant regardless of the contents. I think this basic difference exists and is kind of interesting and maybe it is something to think of when you stage shows that include artists from both worlds. I think I was missing this all of the time.

To come to the actual core of the problem – net.art maybe deserves a bit of an explanation and I'm unable to give you a precise encyclopaedic definition here, but maybe some sort of exploration into what the nature of that particular art practice is would help solve this little detail that essentially curators understand everything but net.art in their own shows. So this is a public call.

SARAH COOK:

I should point out that we've set up this seminar so that today we deal with questions of institutional practice. For instance, Tamas Banovich, who will be talking later today, runs Postmaster's Gallery in New York City and we can look at how he brokers the relationship between the commercial world and the art world. I don't want to create a dichotomy between small and big institutions, but there is a link between size and those that can be very quick on their feet versus those that have to deal with a lot more advanced planning. Tomorrow we've got the opportunity to look more at networked and independent practice.

JULIAN STALLABRASS

SARAH COOK:

Julian Stallabrass is here from London where he teaches at the Courtauld Institute. He curated an exhibition called 'Art and Money Online', which is now on show at Tate Britain.

JULIAN STALLABRASS:

Thanks. I'm not going to speak purely about curatorship – perhaps you will be relieved to hear – but also about the context of the show that I made, 'Art and Money Online'. So the first two thirds of this is really about that context and about issues on the Net and more broadly about art and indeed about 'Art and Money Online'. I'm also going to show you some slides, and I made these slides initially for presentation to art historians so it made them feel comfortable and also because art historians never have Net connections anywhere in their buildings, generally. But having made them I quite like them – this weird, syncretic technology of photographs of Websites. I think they're sweet.

There are perhaps two major aspects to the commercialisation of the online world and one is much more visible than the other. There's first the great increase in the mainstream use of the Internet and the move of corporations into exploitation with browsers and so forth which transformed the Internet from being the realm of academia, state bodies, the military and just being there for a very few technically adept hobbyists, into being a space of mass participation. Yet despite this huge growth, we should remember that this encompasses only a small part of the world's computer-mediated communication systems. The great majority of them are private and as Saskia Sassen, the globalisation writer noted quite recently, just over a quarter of the IP-compatible networks formed the Internet, the rest are locked away in private and proprietary systems.[1]

We will look at one of the works in 'Art and Money Online' that actually takes some steps towards making that system visible. But first here are just a couple of works that respond to some of these issues.

[Slide] This work ('Art and Life', 1999, www.carey young.com/artandlife) is a series of pages by an artist called Carey Young – basically what she did was go out and get some sponsorship. (Here's a nice picture of this cheque being handed over and a picture of the cheque). She then bought shares in two companies called Art and Life, and you can click through various Web pages in which the performance of Art and Life are mapped one against the other in very precise ways. It's just a very clever, pointed intervention I think, especially because in a way it seems ludicrous – the idea that art or life could be valued so precisely and mapped on graphs like this – except that corporations do this all the time in valuing, for

1. Saskia Sassen, 'The Topoi of E-Space: Global Cities and Global Value Chains', in Catherine David and Jean-François Chevrier, eds., Politics-Poetics: Documenta X - The Book, Cantz Verlag, Ostfildern-Ruit 1997, pp. 745.

instance, the commercial value of their art sponsorship. So there's a nice point to this work, I think.

[Slide] I'm sure some of you have seen this – Heath Bunting's 'Internet Beggar'. ('Skint', 1996. www.irational. org/heath/skint) This is just a little piece of text and some boxes and he's asking for money. "Lurking in piss and puke in the stinking alleys of the info-super highway, squatting almost invisibly in piles of corporate data trash – the Internet Beggar, only concerned with his own addictions, tries to blag a dollar off disgusted passers-by...." If you decide to give some money by entering your credit card details, there's a little button you press saying "there you go mate", and "God Bless you sir" appears at the end. He doesn't just put this up on his own irational.org site, but it was pasted into e-mail forums and so people would just come across it unexpectedly and he did indeed get some contributions, although I don't think he dared ever realise them because presumably the credit card numbers were stolen.

VUK COSIC:

Somebody sent him five thousand pounds.

JULIAN STALLABRASS:

Really? Did he actually cash that? Wow! That's amazing. [Slide] And here is a page from ®™ark's fake World Trade Organisation Site (1999, www.gatt.org).

The Web is the public part of a variety of global computer networking systems that have enabled the dramatic growth of the financial markets, which have far out-distanced any other kinds of growths in economic activity.[2] (The UK, incidentally, is in a special position here because its financial economy is not merely larger, but vastly greater than its productive economy – far more so than any other country on the globe, I think).[3] Computer

2. For instance, in 1992 foreign exchange transactions were sixty times larger than world trade. See Saskia Sassen, Losing Control? Sovereignty in an Age of Globalization, Colombia University Press, New York 1996, p. 43.
3. See the figures in Castells. Ref.

communications have played a considerable role in accelerating the neo-liberal global economic system by dramatically easing and lowering the costs of cross-border transactions and services and in the process, undercutting state regulations of national economies.[4] I'm sure this is a picture which is familiar to many of you. Giant transnational companies, particularly in the media and the entertainment sectors, dominate the globalised economy. It may be that technological convergence, globalisation and the concentration of ownership are linked. The economic pressure to make business international leads to companies offsetting the risks of this expansion with mergers and alliances, and these, in their turn, lead to thinking about symbiotic technological crossovers.[5]

One of the major consequences is, of course, the increasing casualisation of labour and while this applies to all sorts of sectors of the economy, the digital industries show the way here. Microsoft was singled out by the Human Rights Watch recently for maltreating its permatemps – people who work for the company but aren't directly employed by them and thus lack insurance, pensions and holidays.[6] Amazon was in trouble with the unions here recently for similarly maltreating its employees in slightly different ways. The IT industry is also at the forefront of prejudice: in the US it employs extremely few Latino and black workers, leading to some firms being fined or sued for racial discrimination or failure to meet federal diversity standards.[7]

But the growth of the Internet has far-reaching implications for the operation of capitalism as a system. Bill Gates has written of 'friction-free capitalism', by which he means that the complete market information that classical

4. This is one of the major themes of Dan Schiller's excellent book, Digital Capitalism: Networking the Global Market System, The MIT Press, Cambridge, Mass. 1999, especially ch. 2.
5. This argument is made in Jill Hills 'The US Rules. OK? Telecommunications Since the 1940s', in Robert W. McChesney/ Ellen Meiksins Wood/ John Bellamy Foster, eds., Capitalism and the Information Age: The Political Economy of the Global Communication Revolution, Monthly Review Press, New York 1998, p. 111.
6. See Julian Borger, 'Workers' Rights "Abused in the US"', The Guardian, 30 August 2000. Microsoft's workforce contains proportionally more of these temps than most companies. See Dan Schiller, Digital Capitalism: Networking the Global Market System, The MIT Press, Cambridge, Mass. 1999, p. 207.
7. See Mike Davis, Magical Urbanism: Latinos Reinvent the US City, Verso, London 2000, pp. 101-2.

economists always assumed was available to buyers and sellers, actually is available to them.[8] Such talk has met with contempt from some postmodern theorists who see it as no more than a fantasy.[9] Yet, I think it's clear that when consumers can compare prices between many companies in a matter of seconds, this is an advance on trawling through the Yellow Pages or tramping down the high street. Indeed, the current tribulations of dot-com companies can partly be blamed on their customers having more price information than is good for profit taking. So to read a bit of Gates' book – 'The Road Ahead' – from 1996:

> "Capitalism, demonstrably the greatest of the constructed economic systems, has in the past decade proved its advantages over the alternative systems. As the Internet evolves into a broadband, global, interactive network, those advantages will be magnified. Products and service providers will see what buyers want a lot more efficiently than ever before and consumers will buy more efficiently. I think Adam Smith would be pleased."[10]

So there are indeed profound and perhaps positive consequences that follow from this integration of economic information into the very structure of production, distribution and consumption, though, as we will see a bit later, they go up way beyond what Gates envisages in this passage.

In the last few years business has been the most publicised aspect of the Internet and there was first the dramatic rise of companies such as Yahoo and Amazon which sustained large losses but had stock valued in billions of dollars. For instance, at the end of the day that Netscape launched itself on the stock market, the company was worth $4.4 billion – which was the largest

8. Bill Gates with Nathan Myhrvold and Peter Rinearson, The Road Ahead, revised edition, Penguin Books, London 1996, ch. 8, especially pp. 180f.
9. See, for example, Slavoj Zizek, The Plague of Fantasies, Verso, London 1997, p.156. Zizek does make the good point that among the frictions eased in Gates' vision is any consideration of social antagonism.
10. Bill Gates with Nathan Myhrvold and Peter Rinearson, The Road Ahead, revised edition, Penguin Books, London 1996, p. 207.

initial public offering in history.[11] More recently of course, there have been spectacular failures with the bankruptcy of once prominent Internet companies and plunging values in the IT sector as a whole. These precipatate rises and falls, founded on a fragile and greatly over-inflated stock market – it's not just the new technology stocks that are in trouble, I think it's a wider problem – shouldn't blind us to the underlying transformation that computer communications bring to the world economy. As I say, it's this intensification of that neo-liberal global process.

Now one area of contention around globalisation is obviously an idea of a national culture. There have been attempts to protect local magazines or films from competition against the products of the world's largest corporations and these run up against World Trade Organisation legislation, which is bent dutifully to fit transnational corporate interests.[12] Search engines and content providers make the Web a more homogenous and governed space than it was. The vast and diverse news and entertainment conglomerates that were assembled through merger from the mid-1980s onwards see the Web as an important platform in which to consolidate their interests.[13] What is of particular concern here is the vertical integration of the Web's layers so that content providers and infrastructure providers are essentially the same people. One of the most publicised mergers is the huge $350 billion merger between AOL and Time-Warner recently, which creates the world's fourth largest corporation.[14] The problem with this vertical integration is obviously the idea that if a company is providing Web services and is running search engines and also providing content, it may well tend to favour its own content above other people's. So the Web becomes a

11. As noted by Tim Berners-Lee (with Mark Fischetti), Weaving the Web: The Past, Present and Future of the World Wide Web by its Inventor, Orion Business Books, London 1999, p. 116.
12. See Dan Schiller, Digital Capitalism: Networking the Global Market System, The MIT Press, Cambridge, Mass. 1999, pp. 79f.
13. This point is made by Dan Schiller, Digital Capitalism: Networking the Global Market System, The MIT Press, Cambridge, Mass. 1999, p. 99.
14. For an analysis, see Jane Martinson, A Media Giant Caught in the Web', The Guardian, 11 January 2000.

somewhat different space than it appears, or was initially anticipated to be.

Web users are analysed as they surf and valuable data is mined from their behaviour so as to better to target adverts and other commercial material at them. And the Net is the ideal surveillance tool, the object being to register every consumer whim and to cater instantly to it – indeed, to eventually anticipate the whim, to satisfy it before it is fully formed.[15] Slavoj Zizek, pressing upon the conclusion of this process and one which, it must be said, is very remote from the current experience of Net users, the boundaries between the living and the artificial, between objective reality and its appearance are undermined and the identity of the perceiving self perishes:

"Potentially total subjectivisation (the reduction of reality to an electro-mechanically generated cyberspace 'window') coincides with total objectivisation (the subordination of our 'inner' bodily rhythm to a set of stimulations regulated by external apparatuses)."[16]

So he thinks the abolition of distance will also be the abolition of neighbourliness; universal availability will induce 'unbearable claustrophobia'; excess choice will breed an inability to choose: in all, the vision of cyberspace leads to radical closure and 'an infinity far more suffocating than any actual confinement.'[17] Well it's a bleak and compelling vision, but one, as I say, which is very far removed from any current reality.

[Slide] This is rather an old atlas of cyberspace which simply maps, quite crudely, not just regional traffic, but traffic between nations.

Well, the first thing to say about this vision of Zizek's – who is it for, who are these people who are going to be immediately satisfied in this way? There are a couple of myths about the online audience. It is large, but ninety-five

15. I published a text on this subject: 'Formas de la identitad en el ciberespacio' [Being Yourself in Cyberspace], Revista de Occidente, no. 206, June 1998, pp. 77-97.
16. Slavoj Zizek, The Plague of Fantasies, Verso, London 1997, p. 135.
17. Ibid., p. 154.

per cent of the world's population are not online, so in one way it is large and if looked at in another way, it is small. It is quite geographically concentrated too. Obviously the States accounts for a very large chunk of online users and particular bits of the States as well and I think you know where they are. There are many, many areas where the Internet has yet to make much, if any, impact at all.

Both the rise of Internet Art and the rise of online commerce were founded upon the Web browser and are broadly coincident. The two are often opposed, but are also sometimes bound up tightly with one another. As Josephine Berry has pointed out, Net artists have had to deal with the tension between, in a sense, the radical potential of the Net, which many people have heavily invested in, and its increasingly conservative commercial use.[18] Commercialisation on the Web produces a uniformity of its look. This is a matter of browsers now dominated by Internet Explorer, themselves based upon another design standard, Windows, with its scroll bars and windows within windows. But also of other specifically online standard ephemera, if you like – frames, banner advertising, animated GIFs, rollover effects and so on.[19]

So we see a tendency of an homogenised Web to become, one could argue, an over-arching commodity itself and this very much works against the more ideal images of the Web as a forum or a library. It's also to do with the desktop, which, within limits, makes the screen an office environment, and the user an employee. Although work and leisure are only ever a window or a click away in this environment, I think, despite the sharp distinctions, there is a movement between the two that is incredibly easy. It's a matter that Theodor Adorno would have recognised in his writings about work and leisure, and under capitalism and the cultural industries – their

18. Josephine Berry, 'The Thematics of Site-specific Art on the Net', Manchester, 2001. To be published at www.metamute.com
19. This point is made by Steven Johnson, Interface Culture: How New Technology Transforms the Way we Create and Communicate, Basic Books, New York 1997, p. 93.

secret affinity. He says that one of the reasons that they appear to be divided off so sharply is to disguise something like a secret affinity between them.

To think about the conventions of the commercial Web page a bit – there are parallels to be drawn with the design of magazine pages (particularly with leisure magazines and art, fashion and lifestyle magazines which seem to be coming closer and closer together) – magazines which integrate editorial and advertising material to the degree that the two can no longer be sharply distinguished.[20] Both use visual and verbal information acting together, both are intended to convey condensed hits of information. Now as it is, advertisers lean on the offline media – papers, magazines, TV companies – to ensure that their messages are not disrupted by inconvenient facts or disturbing news stories.[21] This is absolutely regular practice and by far the largest form of institutional censorship in the mass media comes from advertisers and not governments and this applies even more, I think, to standard Web pages. Net technology has been used to bring about a tighter integration of advertising and publicity content with other material. So the danger in all this is that the uniformity of look and interface creates a uniformity and passivity of behaviour among Net users. As commercialisation gathers apparently unstoppable impetus, various prominent Net activists, including Heath Bunting, Geert Lovink and Critical Art Ensemble, suggested that the battle was already lost – this was in the late nineties.[22] Here's Lovink in 1998:

"Against all expectations the Internet is creating a new mass of 'users' that just shut up and click/listen. They are 'watching Internet' – a phrase that would have been impossible to come up with a few years ago. This silent majority in the making, which will only

20. Paul Zelevansky, 'Shopping on the Home Image Network', Art Journal, vol. 56, Fall 1997, pp. 46-7.
21. For an account of some recent scandals of advertisers determining copy, see Dan Schiller, Digital Capitalism: Networking the Global Market System, The MIT Press, Cambridge, Mass. 1999, 124-5.
22. As pointed out by J.J. King, 'Bringing it all Back Home: Life on the New Flesh Frontier', Mute, no. 12, p.49.

know the red 'Buy' button, was not envisioned by the early adapters and visionaries of the first hour."[23]

Now perhaps those sentiments may have been over-hasty, but I think they capture the drama of the change involved on the Web as Web use erupted. Yet, just as cultural homogenisation in its spread of chain stores, movies and pop songs across the globe provokes sharp local resistance and serves, in many cases, to delineate the borders of other identities and of activism itself, so the wave of online commercialisation did the same. The Net became the place to find anti-corporate information and organise anti-corporate activities.[24] Even for Gates, the free market and data cannot by itself be guaranteed to produce what he calls "an undistorted picture of the market". Gates is very worried that the Web is used for all this stuff – he thinks that somehow all these opinions carry too much weight within the Web. Of course, Microsoft has a large share of people who are pissed off with it and advertise their grudges on the Web. Indeed, in this book he wants some unspecified tool for reducing the volume of these voices of what he calls 'libel or slander', whilst somehow protecting freedom of expression. Yet such complaints or sites devoted to the proposition that some corporation or other sucks, are the specific end of a continuum of anti-corporate and anti-capitalist opinion that's found a means of transmission on the Net, excluded as it was from the mainstream media for so long – certainly for twenty years or more.

So I think a lot of Internet Art works against this background of commercialisation by making itself distinct, by frustrating the expectations of users who are used to familiar ways in which programmes look and behave.

[Slide] This is a page from Jodi's site and I imagine many of you know this (www.jodi.org). There are sites that spurn fancy design, sites that are – in rather a Brechtian

23. Geert Lovink, nettime mailing, 21 July 1998; cited in J.J. King, 'Bringing it all Back Home: Life on the New Flesh Frontier', Mute, no. 12, p. 49.
24. See for example the site condemning McDonalds (www.mscpotlight.org).

way, as in Jodi – highlighting the making of Web pages and doing unusual things with them, and sites which play with expectations over hyperlinks – either not using them at all or putting in so many that they become impossible to follow.

[Slide] These are a few images from Rachel Baker's 'Dot-to-Dot' (1997, www.irational.org/tm/dot2dot), which is quite a nice site that leads users to expect the downloading of pornographic pictures and then frustrates that expectation.

[Slide] Another famous and commonly used tactic is the creation of fake Web pages, as we've seen with ®™ark's false World Trade Organisation pages which were up at the time of the Seattle demonstrations against them. Another nice site that they did was about IBM's technological role in the Holocaust.

[Slide] This is their false George W. Bush site, made at the time of the elections (1999, www.gwbush.com). Bush in this particular page is saying that he's a very forgiving politician because he understands the mistakes that people have made in the past and it lists a few of them. This is a reference to Bush's rather colourful youth.

Anti-commercial sentiment on the Web achieved a dramatic expression in February 2000 when successful blocking attacks were launched against some of the most prominent commercial sites, including CNN, Yahoo, eBay and Amazon. They were perhaps less an articulate critique of mass commerce than a cry of protest that for a short time blocked out all else. In an often prescient set of lectures published as 'Art and Technics' in 1952, Lewis Mumford outlined the hypertrophied worship of technology that leads to both over-rationalism in some areas and, as compensation, wildly subjective reactions in others. He says:

"In this impersonal and over-disciplined machine civilisation, so proud of its objectivity, spontaneity too often takes the form of criminal acts and creativity finds its main outlet in destruction."[25]

Indeed, this is, I think, the recourse of some of those who are dissatisfied with a seemingly universal system of administration; one that has so far quite effectively blocked out the development of coherent alternatives, even in the mind, within its very rapid assimilation of all that would lie outside its ambit. [...]

I think sometimes there comes to be art and political crossovers here, which would be pretty much unthinkable in the gallery or mainstream art world. Just as an example, the online artists' centre Backspace in London, hosted the site that carried information about the 'J18 day of action' that saw anti-capitalist demonstrations take over the City of London in 1999.[26] I think that's an alliance that you would not often find in gallery or museum practice, to say the least. I think that both online and offline, you're getting a sometimes fascinating fusion of political and cultural actions so that it's hard to tell when one ends and where one begins. I mean, offline I think this is definitely true of groups like 'Reclaim the Streets', which use performance art and even elements of installation art as practical political tools.[27]

So I think what I'm going to do is move into talking about the show ['Art and Money Online'] a bit because I think you've got the basic background to it now. As I said, it falls within this general context. I curated what turned out to be quite a small show at Tate Britain. I was on a fellowship there for a year with Paul Mellon funding and it was an Art Now show, so it was shown – for those of you who haven't seen the exhibition – in that small room at the end of Tate Britain. It's a ghettoised contemporary art space and there were three works in it which, I hope,

25. Lewis Mumford, Art and Technics, University of Columbia Press, New York 1952, pp. 10-11.
26. See http://bak.spc.org/j18/site/
27. See the essay on the M11 link road campaign by Aufheben, in George McKay, ed., DIY Culture: Party & Protest in Nineties Britain, Verso, London 1998.

each made quite distinct statements about this state of affairs, focusing on private financial networks, on the commercial vulgarisation of Net culture and also looking at an alternative online culture of sharing and gift-giving.

[Slide] Imagine looking up at a night sky that is also a live representation of the global stock market. Each star represents a traded company, with the largest being the brightest and stars cluster together or drift apart, glowing strongly or faintly and changing colour, depending on the movement of their stocks. Within this environment digital creatures – a form of artificial life – navigate the star field, feeding off the trading, much the same as stockbrokers do and evolving, becoming more efficient as they go. These creatures can die from lack of food if they're not efficient enough in finding it, or if they find enough to get the energy and breed with other creatures, they produce children. So there's an element of evolution working here. This was a work called 'Black Shoals/Stock Market Planetarium' (2001, www.blackshoals.net) by Lise Autogena, a Danish artist, and Joshua Portway. It works on a number of levels. Part of it is to do with a quite postmodern, indeed Jamesonian take on mapping – on the aspiration but also the impossibility to map the complex systems that we create and which take on their own emergent order. As I say, one of the things that this work does is to make visible the usually invisible and un-visualis-able movements of stocks on the global exchanges. But I think there's also something about the way this work is shown on a dome in a darkened space in Tate Britain, so you look up to it. It's rather like looking up at a night sky. There's also something about it that's quite mystical or astrological – an engagement with this realm of distant cosmic effects which we look to for a sign – you know, we try to read signs into it all the time. Except, of course, this is a world which absolutely does have an effect over all our lives whether we want it to or not, so perhaps it's more astronomy than astrology.

There's another, curious aspect to this work which is that obviously if you can come up with a visualisation of the stock market which allows pattern recognition – even stockbrokers who are very well trained at looking at rows and rows of figures are not necessarily very good at finding patterns in them, in fact they're quite slow in doing that – then this could be an instrumental tool in globalisation in making capitalism more efficient. As could the artificial life creatures; nobody knows in fact what they will do. Will they become efficient enough to actually predict changes in this environment? The work has an ambivalence and a double-edge, I think. Part of it, as I said, is about our own fantasies about the difficulties of mapping the postmodern sphere, but there's a more instrumental edge to it as well and I think that's quite interesting.

[Slide] Jon Thomson and Alison Craighead did a piece called 'CNN Interactive Just Got More Interactive' (2001, www.thomson-craighead.net), which is a version of something that they'd already done on the Web and basically what this piece does is to provide a soundtrack for the CNN Website. Now this is actually a live Web screen and people can browse out from it if they want to. How do we control that? Well, the piece resets itself every fifteen minutes and goes back to the homepage, but there's nothing to stop people browsing quite far out from where it starts. The soundtrack remains; it's a light blue bar across the top of the browser. You can choose different mood music from disaster or catastrophe through to jubilant music. Thomson & Craighead have long been mining the weird mix of participatory and corporate culture which you find on the Net. They make pieces which approach online anthropology – holding up the bizarre habits of Net users to the art audience. I think this particular work, which is a very simple but effective intervention, presses on the worry that it's increasingly difficult to pick apart the two halves of infotainment, especially on the Web where, as I've said, another distraction is only ever a click or a frame away and where entertainment, commercial content and editorial are merged.

[Slide] The last piece was by Redundant Technology Initiative – a group of artists based in Sheffield who, as their name suggests, are concerned with the truly extraordinary waste of the computer industry (www.lowtech.org). Machines are rendered apparently useless in the space of a few years, long before the end of their components' lifespan. Redundant Technology Initiative persuades companies to give them their 'old' machines and use them either for works of art or for their community computer space. Using donated machines and free, Open Source software, they come quite close to achieving their goal of what they call 'no cost technology'.

RTI are best known for stand-alone banks of computer monitors and installations using disassembled computer components, but they have recently been using work that draws on the Web. This was a piece called 'Free Agent' (2001). It was partly using video which was shot in a shopping centre – again focusing in on the word 'free' – but also using material taken from Websites offering free material. So here reclaimed hardware and free software are directed at sites which desperately, if dubiously, offer the user something for nothing. Obviously their model of free stuff is very, very different from that commercial offer. In a way it shows that the art practice and the computer centre and RTI's process of recycling technology are connected; they are all part of the same project. I think they were very pleased about coming to the Tate because it was a good propaganda exercise for them and they expected to get lots of machines out of it. One of the nice things that happened actually was that the Tate itself was disposing of thirty or so machines and they gave them to RTI. These machines, although they were old, were better than anything that RTI had in their computing space, so they've managed to refit the computing space completely. I'm very pleased with that result, I must say.

Now these works are obviously hybrid works and they were commissioned for the show. Part of the idea of the show was to create something of a crossover audience between those people who knew about online culture and Web art and those people who know about gallery and museum art. They are two connected elites, but very often the crossover is not – as Vuk has already suggested – as close as it might be. So that was part of the aim of the show; it was meant, in many ways, to be an educative show. But of course, works like this are very different from pure Web art. You can easily make copies of that and many pieces of online art works are gifts to their viewers; they don't have a material presence. The code can be reused and very often it is and plainly that kind of work is very different from the sorts of work that we're mostly familiar with. They are different from even the most radical works of conceptual art, which I think they follow on from in a certain sense and which retain some sliver of materiality that was seized upon as they were drawn into mainstream art institutions. The ownership and status of online works, I think, is a really difficult matter for the art world, sunk as it is in ancient craft practices and habits of patronage. Even more terrifying perhaps than the sharing of music files is for the music industry, because as Eric Hobswan points out, the art world has not yet embraced mechanical reproduction fully, never mind the next stage.

So 'Art and Money Online' was a way of exploring that interaction between the online art world and the museum. Each potentially has things to offer the other: the museum brings to online artists, audiences that they otherwise might find hard to reach, for it's easy to languish in obscurity when the Web is full of brash and rich commercial sites; online artists clearly give the museum a link into a rapidly changing and alien culture. But there is a real worry that as other new media, like photography and video for instance, became accommodated by the museum, many would say that they changed too much in their transformation into familiar-looking works of art and the museum didn't change enough. But the challenge of online art is greater and it holds out the hope for a transformation of art in a democratic and participatory direction. I think I would strongly endorse what Vuk said about conversations in the online world and the importance and the openness of those. I think there's such a difference between the mainstream art world and the online world in that way and it's one of the most striking contrasts. So as I say, there's a potential here for the transformation of art in a democratic and participatory direction, but the resistance in the art institutions, and above all the art market, will be strong and dangerous.

[Slide] There were two panels when you went into the exhibition. One, once you had got inside the door to the Art Now room, I had written and was my opinion of what the show was about. But the other one – before you went through that door, which said 'Sponsor' at the top and which I hadn't seen until the show opened – was rather extraordinary. Now part of what this says is how wonderful Reuters is – and that's fine. That's what you would expect and they did give quite a bit of money to the show. What this does raise very clearly is that there was one installation – Autogena's and Portway's – which required a lot of money and so I think that immediately involves you in certain compromises which RTI, as I said, steps around. But the other thing that this panel does is to give Reuters' idea of what's going on in the exhibition – as if they had been in some way responsible for its curation – and that I did find rather extraordinary. Their view of it was much more upbeat, in a sense, than mine.

So I guess the question that I want to end with is whether, in a show like this, the educative and access virtues of it – I hope they are virtues – outweigh the contamination of pure Net Art through its potential commodification, and the training that the mainstream art world gets in bending Net Art to its purposes? As I say, I really don't know. I was saying to Sarah earlier that for me, doing this show, which is the first show that I've curated, was a form of education – perhaps rather a peculiar one – but as I say, whether in fact, in making this show. I contributed to a process that I would be very much against is a question I'm not sure about. So I'll end there.

[Audience applause]

HANNAH REDLER:

Prior to joining the C-PLEX project I was working for the National Museum of Photography, Film and Television in Bradford, and then The Science Museum in London. In both places I was working on delivering digital galleries that included, or were led by, artists' installations and obviously issues of dealing with Web art came into it. I think that one of the schisms we've got at the moment is that the Internet is an emerging form, which is probably something that you've come up against and suddenly you've got the Tate and the Science Museum trying to show something as a finished product, but in fact the debate and the discussion that's going on in the creation of the works isn't a finished product. I think a lot of the works that you've talked about are works that seem to be more successful and are often the ones where artists are undermining the corporate occupation of cyberspace. But there's also a whole area of artistic research around use and socialisation of Web space that isn't being shown in institutions, because, in my experience, we really don't know how. There are lots of reasons why we don't know how and one of them was Vuk's point, that you just can't take an intimate work, something that's meant to be seen on the small screen, and project it like The Whitney Museum did in the 2000 Biennial. Large-scale is boring! It's not an interesting exhibition experience and I think there are also questions to be asked about when people come to museums and art galleries – are they looking for a curated, edited experience? I think they are, so in that respect we don't want people to go whizzing off to the porn sites – they can do that at home. But on the other hand, we don't want them to feel that we're being over authoritative, so I think it's quite difficult. I don't think we should be looking for fixed answers. I think it's still a really strong area for research.

JULIAN STALLABRASS:

Yes, I think there are lot of good points there. When the Tate was thinking about a larger show for this – maybe a three-roomed exhibition – what I wanted to do was to have maybe the middle room just as an Internet Café which people could use for free. But I feel extremely uncomfortable about this hobbling of browsers that you often get, or the removal of online content completely so that it all comes cached from a hard disk or whatever. At the ZKM (Zentrum für Kunst und Medientechnologie, Karlsruhe) I had this very strange experience of having to move from machine to machine to see different works, as if it was pictures in a gallery. I mean, this is surely absurd! It's crazy. My position on [security] would be to say you can allow people access to recommended works, but I think you must not control them. I think that you've just got to allow them to do what they want in the end and if the museum is useful in this – and maybe it is just not – perhaps you can provide at least a space where people can be comfortable and relaxed and not too surveilled. In terms of providing access in that way, it could be useful. But maybe the museum is not the place for this? I don't know. I think the point about process was very important. There were certainly some people at the Tate who didn't get RTI. They looked at it and they said, 'Oh, God! That's so awful, sort of 1960s video art. It looks horrible and we don't like it aesthetically.' But they absolutely, completely missed the point that for RTI that's a stage in an ongoing process and that's something that was quite difficult to get across to some people.

STEVEN BODE:

I just wanted to talk a bit about the curatorial decision-making process that's been part of the Tate show. I think I'm right in saying that every other 'Art Now' show at the Tate has always been a showcase of a single artist – well, most, if not all of them have. I just wondered whose decision it was to include three works in the show – whether it had come from you or whether there had been an implicit pressure from the Tate? Because often what happens with work which institutions feel slightly less than confident about, is the sense that maybe the work won't stand up on its own so they need to give people a bit more of that just in case they don't like that piece. I went to see it the other week and I just felt that the 'Black Shoals' piece was so good in embodying the ideas that you were talking about in 'Art and Money Online' that it felt that everything else had been slightly crowded in on top of that. I was thinking of seeing Fiona Banner or Thomas Demand in the 'Art Now' gallery – neither of which completely filled the space. The Tate wouldn't have dared to say, 'Thomas, we really like your piece, but we think another piece by another artist would give a more fulfilling experience for someone.' I just wondered whether that decision had come via you or whether you felt that there was some implicit pressure to make it more of a group show or a showcase show?

JULIAN STALLABRASS:

Well the pressure was actually in the opposite direction. The Tate were very impressed earlier on by the Autogena and Portway piece and would, I think, have been quite happy to show that on its own and so I was actually being constantly pressured to reduce the number of artists in the show. I was extremely reluctant to do that because of the proposal that I had originally put to them. The question about the size of the show and whether it was perhaps going to be one, two or three rooms – once you start working in an institution like that you realise how dependent on other things decisions like that are: on other shows, last minute changes in Tate schedules, things like that. So this exhibition was obviously a fairly low priority for them, I think. And it got messed around as a result. If you go to the Tate and walk through the Duveen Galleries, before you get to the 'Art and Money Online' gallery – this is now a typical Tate 'hanger' thing – there are vast amounts of empty space. There are yards and yards between the sculptures. They were very resistant to me crowding things into that room. Maybe they are right. Maybe you felt that it was a bit crowded, but the main worries for them were, 'Oh, we must give these works space to breathe.' They would have been happier with a monographic show, I think. It would have fitted into the tenor of what they were doing. The other thing I should say about this show is that it's the first time, although Art Now is their project space, that artists who haven't had dealer representation have ever shown there. In fact, Carey Young presented a brilliant proposal for this show and I would have loved to have had her in it as well, but for reasons of space I couldn't.

VUK COSIC:

Just to try and not really answer what you've asked in the end, but I've been around this net.art thing since that afternoon it started. There was this way of thinking at the beginning that finally we've got a system where we're absolutely not dependent on the state, curators or the military, and it was nice. We had, similar to the video people, total control over the means of production in our hands, but also over distribution for the first time – so we were free. And only much later, the art world became interesting or interested, which is more scary. What should be said is that first, this little group of net.art people, we were all thirty or so years old when we started. It was not a thing done by some teenagers just out of art school. We all had experiences. Alexi Shulgin was a successful photographer travelling around the globe with his show. Jodi was doing video, I was doing totally other stuff, and Heath Bunting was Heath Bunting! Anyway, we already had our experiences and everyone knows we had a bit of an attitude towards the art world. And later on we somehow started doing things together somewhere in Kassel (at Documenta). Usually people ask me, 'how come you gave in so quickly?' Well maybe this is an answer to your question of how Net art loses by educating or informing the art world about how things are. What I keep saying in these public appearances is that ... well the right question would be, 'how come these two are coming together at all? Why?' I usually say there are two reasons. One is the biggest force in the universe, which is the conformism of the artists, and the second, is the need for the museums to maintain their prestige and they do it only by showing actual contemporary art. Now the conformism of the artist is bringing us this thing that we've already seen – some of us who are old enough to remember the early days of video where you had these people working very hard on monitors trying to say to us that that's the only pure video art, and then those who were more eager to adapt were doing projections. We ended up with Bill Viola – really beautiful, painterly videos and all they are missing is the frame.

The other detail is regarding the maintenance of prestige (I think I was mentioning before how it works and why). What I observe as especially revolting are these totally drunken marriages between arts institutions and technological firms. I think the most extreme example was

SUN-ICA, this institution in London that recently changed its name back into ICA. It's terrible. But then you have a far more intelligent case in the US. You have SFMoMA, that's owned by the Intel Corporation. You can see that in this recent show ('010101: Art in Technological Times', SFMoMA, 2001). It is dreadful because usually those marriages are done because some decision-makers believe that this other institution, just by being famous for its ability to sell lots of machines, also has the knowledge. So if you look today at what the ICA actually achieved... come on! They got two aquariums for unused and useless machines and they sold their shop window across the street from Buckingham Palace to some Americans – how cool! No single artist profited out of this. No single artist went to California to work with engineers to think of, create and invent some good tools, which I think would be a very cool thing for artists to do in life. So this is how that process really looks for me and this is why I also think it will go on because there's this terrible need for conformism and prestige.

JULIAN STALLABRASS:

What you say explains quite well what the attraction is for the art institutions, but what's the attraction for somebody like you? Or not to make it so personal, why do Net artists play along?

VUK COSIC:

Well, as I said, because conformism is the biggest force in the universe. I just like being in those grand slam places, you know. I've been to all these places and my mum is so proud! [Laughter]. I've had a show in every museum that she's ever heard of! Just now I did this thing in the Guggenheim in Venice and now she's one really proud mother. Plus, I'm trying to have a day job where I earn money so I don't have to do art, so I'm doing commercial Websites hoping that it will bring in more money, but it isn't for the moment. I'm trying to get out. It's like those stories, 'I wanted to study economy or law, but my mother wouldn't let me and she made me study art.' It's one of those situations. One of the reasons that you do art in life is possibly to influence people and by getting exposed you're getting a better chance – I would say. Depending on what you want to say.

JULIAN STALLABRASS:

Yes, yes exactly.

PAMELA WELLS:

Going back to this idea about artists making Websites who are not necessarily making it for that kind of public engagement in a museum or art gallery, and going back to the idea that when you curate a show that's mostly Websites – part of me just wonders is there or isn't there a way that you can curate it? You were saying that you can't quite curate it so you just don't; it's okay if people start with an art Website and then they go off somewhere else. I wonder if that's not just lazy curating? Because there has to be some way to mitigate the bridge between artists creating Websites for a very private experience, in your home, and showing that work in a gallery. Surely there must be a way to not just reset it every fifteen minutes, so then we don't care if they go to porn sites. From the perspective of a youth arts organisation, we'd lose our funding in a heartbeat! I'm wondering whether there has to be some kind of curatorial 'control' (for lack of a better term), not just say, 'we can't curate it so we won't.'

JULIAN STALLABRASS:

I think the problem is not just of authoritarianism but if you take works which are meant to be seen on the Web and you take the environment of the Web out of there, you're doing a good deal to destroy them, I think. That's the fundamental problem. There are certainly technical ways of getting around people not visiting porn sites if that is what pisses you off in particular. But I think it is not that you abrogate your responsibility entirely. As I said, there are ways of presenting work for people, to present it to them to say, 'this is something that you should look at.' But then, what they do with that work, where they go from that work, I think maybe you do have to leave to them; I'm not sure.

JOASIA KRYSA:

I have a different question, perhaps of a different nature. You mentioned earlier the cultural industry concept, coined originally by the Frankfurt school. But they didn't originally include art – it referred more to mass media, TV, press, radio. Would you see today, with the impact of digital technologies, digital art as a part of this concept? And if so, by what conditions?

JULIAN STALLABRASS:

I was using the cultural industry to refer to commercial culture online, I suppose. I think plainly a lot of Web artists – in an eerily familiar way, in an almost avant-gardist way – are resisting the impetus of the cultural industry. And in a way, oddly, that Adorno would have found quite familiar, there is something about strains of Net art which are quite autonomous and specialist and very much caught up in their own concerns, and that's another way, perhaps, of blocking out that noise of commercial culture. I think there may well be good arguments for saying that the mainstream art world is now a minor part of the cultural industry. That same kind of separation that Greenberg saw and recommended is not in place anymore. I think that's true.

HANNAH REDLER:

Just to say, although I don't think necessarily the Tate or the Science Museum or any of these big organisations are the best place for showing work, I do think they can act as brokers. This is something I am talking about with the Science Museum and it is very interested in using its relationship with industry and its position in government – I hope! – to make opportunities more available for artistic research. And I think this whole thing of media art as having a more healthy discourse about art with a social agenda, art in context with society, is something that the mainstream art world has a lot to learn from. I mean, it is one of the reasons I work with media art, because I found the mainstream art world very frustrating and limiting. Thinking of creative ways of building conversations and expanding on this discourse to wider audiences is, I think, something that we can do.

VUK COSIC:

May I say a word about showing and curating online stuff in a gallery space? There is one detail that somehow I failed to mention before. In my view, when you show online stuff in a gallery space, which is not online, you essentially put it in the wrong place. It's not at home. It's not where it is supposed to be. It's decontextualised; it's shown in a glass test-tube. So whatever you do is just an attempt to make it look more alive. You either move the test-tube or have some fancy lighting. And this is how it works for me. If actual curating of online stuff can only be done online, it is done by everybody alive and it is called 'links'. And if you are able to draw enough attention, as a quality broker of dialogue about quality ideas, you will get very many people visiting your curatorial site. And they will be visiting the links you have put there. I think that is actually curating of online media, period. But if you want to involve physical spaces (and I think that is the topic of this discussion in actual fact), then have to go for some trade-offs, and one of them is this here question, whether or not you allow for porn celebrities to show up in your gallery spaces. [Laughter] You can also decide to do, like the Kassel people did at Documenta in 1997, to make an office with desks and computers on top and then paint one wall in black and say it is anti-IBM and therefore anti-corporate – come on! I think their shares dropped dramatically that afternoon! I mean there is a lot of bluffing going on.

SARAH COOK:

I feel a need every time I get involved in this sort of discussion about gallery space and curatorial issues as regards new media art online to mention that the new media department at the Walker Art Center in Minneapolis – which is widely viewed as one of the first museums to really support online art practices – have their offices in what used to be a bathroom; they have no real estate whatsoever. We (museums) rush forward so quickly to secure relationships with different corporate bodies or different funding agencies in order to give artists the kind of gallery presentation recognition that they need and yet maybe we need to slow down and take these baby steps first of all; not think so much about the hardware and just start with what the artists need and figure how can we provide that on that base level. And if it is converting an old bathroom so that you've got a desk in there, then that's a good start.

TAMAS BANOVICH

SARAH COOK:

I'd like to introduce Tamas Banovich who has just arrived from New York, where he runs Postmasters Gallery.

TAMAS BANOVICH:

Good afternoon, my name is Tamas Banovich and at this point in my life I wear several hats, one of which is being the curator of new media programming at our gallery. The other is that I am still trying to do some semi-independent curating. And the third one, which I will talk about later, is experimenting with possible forms of the economy of art, in this case being a part of a corporation, a company. So there are some obvious conflicts of interest one could say that might become apparent, but I can live with it.

Just very briefly my background – I was born in Hungary but studied in Poland. I graduated from the Warshaw Academy of Art in 1977. My interest was sculpture and space and so-called habitat / living space design and theatre design. The reason I am saying this is because it might become relevant at various points. I moved to New York in 1980 and in 1985 my partner, Magdalena Sawon and I, started Postmasters Gallery. I think the concept of an art gallery is a little different in the United States than here. It [Postmasters] is a commercial gallery representing a group of artists; it is a business. Its only income comes from the sale of art or income from various art activities. Ninety-nine per cent of it is from the sale of art objects. So this is framing and defining what we do, what we can and cannot do. But the obvious advantage of it is that since it is a private enterprise, we can really do whatever we want. Both of us came from Eastern Europe and I would say we have a very underdeveloped sense of business, but we were fiercely independent and individualistic and this was the only forum where we could do what we wanted to do. And the focus of what we wanted to do was to participate in contemporary culture and that is how we formed the gallery.

The gallery was formed in 1985, during the renaissance of artistic activity in New York. It was when the East Village opened up: a part of the city where, after years of very limited access for upcoming artists in established galleries, suddenly, because of an ongoing economic boom, it was possible to start new venues. Most of these were started by artists themselves to create new venues in which to exhibit their art. In a very short period there were eighty new galleries formed in that area.

Originally our programme was focused on what we called 'thinking art'. Right before that there was a period of neo-expressionist art and we couldn't identify with that; we wanted to propose something else. And so the practice of the artists we engaged in a dialogue with, ranged from hardcore conceptual art to art which focused on cultural and contemporary issues. With time, the programme loosened up and we gained confidence in what we were doing. Our driving force was to show what we think is relevant and interesting in contemporary art and culture. We are part of a community – a close community like everywhere else, but relatively large, very international and open. Sometimes we do things in reaction to what is going on in the world or what is going on at the time in New York.

My role in the gallery at the beginning was a background role. Magda is an art historian and it was her dream to start the gallery. My role was to maintain the relationships with the artists, and I was arranging and designing the exhibitions. I have always been interested in the psychology of space and so I had the opportunity this way to work with some of my ideas and understand how the work is received and perceived. It, in itself, is very satisfying work because I soon discovered that the space and the arrangement of the work and the way you present it is fundamental in influencing how it is received and understood. Part of this process is to understand what the artist's intention is and then try to translate it and make it legible for the public.

In 1994 or 1995 I was struck by the fact that there was this huge cultural change going on – that technology changed how people interact, work and how they perceive the world and this somehow wasn't reflected in the art of the time. I certainly wasn't involved in the beginnings of media art (what was happening in Ars Electronica, Siggraph and all these places). I think it was because I was following this obviously ignorant rule of thumb that everything that is connected to technology is 'gadgety' technology and distracts artists from concentrating their concepts and ideas down to their essence.

So I became interested and the first incident was very weird. I knew an artist in New York who was a very interesting artist – he had had a couple of shows, he was very promising, as they say. And then suddenly he disappeared. After a couple of years, I asked some people what had happened to him. I was told, 'he's on the

Internet.' And so I went to visit him – his house was full of computers and modems and wiring and he was spending hundred of dollars on Internet services. I spent six hours with him that day because I wanted to find out what he was doing and what it was about the Internet that excited him. So we spent six hours trying to get on the Net, and when we got a connection, going to a few sites, trying to navigate them. And that was it. After six hours I realised his excitement was that he could surf the Net and go to various sites and communicate with people via e-mail; he was absorbed by the process and that was shocking, and at the same time fascinating, to me. Because he was totally obsessed – that was his whole life. And I realised that if I started to explore the Web without a purpose, I would probably do the same thing he was doing. So I decided that if I was to learn about the Web, I would use it to understand first and then somehow represent this phenomena, create an exhibition out of it. At the time it was a totally ignorant notion on my part because I had no clue what was going on.

So I spent the next year and a half surfing the Web, corresponding with people and artists and basically my initial impression was that this was not a technology, but a new medium being born. That made me more excited because I was fascinated with technology but I did not want it to be the focus of my interest or of this endeavour. The thought that I could be present at the birth of this medium and somehow contribute to that was very fascinating. So I came to this conclusion and I saw that there were other things going on – especially in Europe – Rhizome was born at the time, and serious artists were trying to master this medium. My idea was that, if this was a new medium, then what would be interesting would be to find people for whom this was their first medium. Not artists who have an art education and who were educated in another medium, but artists for whom this is their primary medium of expression. So I separated myself from the New York art world and was exclusively trying to find these people on the Web. And so the next challenge was to present this. I was looking for a unifying form that could represent this medium and at the time I had the idea that it was the screensaver: a short work that had a random structure, some were interactive, and all introduced the loop. These were elements which were interesting and made the medium different from what other mediums could do. So I decided to do a show that would be a screensaver show. I invited a lot of people. A lot of them were not artists at all; some of them were hackers, and when I wrote to them that I considered their work art, they were stupefied by that idea. I also started to have a large network of friends who were designers – especially on the West Coast – where everything was five or ten years ahead and generations had already grown up very close to technology. The whole culture was built around technology in an extreme way – from San Diego to Seattle – with huge communities which were way ahead in using and understanding technology, much more than anywhere else in the world, except perhaps Finland. So I started to work with this bunch of people. What I wanted to focus on was the challenges of working with new media.

What emerged from this whole experience was first of all a realisation that I was never in love with the art world system. I didn't like the fact that the only form of our economy was to sell objects and that meant that you either couldn't deal with a form of art that didn't lend itself to that, or it forced you to find a material representation of everything. It was obviously ridiculous in the context of electronic art where the whole idea was of the virtual and immaterial (at least at that time it seemed like that). So that was already one problem. Another one of the things I didn't like about the art world was its tendency to force its structure on the artists. For us, the focus was to work with and represent the artists and their ideas, obviously in the context of what we were doing. So from the very beginning we were looking for another structure through which we could function. But all other structures, like non-profit, still looked less attractive to us. So obviously there were serious challenges there – how to represent it and how to convince people who are interested in art that it has a lasting value. How to get the idea through that they should support this kind of activity and participate in creating a different economy through these things.

So, suddenly we were faced with a different set of people in many ways – the 'new' artist. They were totally isolated and they had no clue about the structure of the art world. It sounds superficial but that's the truth. We were used to dealing with people that by the time they got to a gallery understood the system, they were even playing the system, trying to crack it. And suddenly there were these people who, because they were excluded from the system, were basically oblivious to it. They were ghettoised into these festivals and had no interaction with artists who worked in other mediums. And also there was this thought that basically they do not need the mediation that the art world provides because their work is available on the Web. It sounded very seductive to me at the time and I almost believed it. But the history and progress of the Web changed the whole situation very fast. When I started, you could find everyone and every site because there were so few of them and everybody was actively looking and reaching out for works because there was little else interesting there. But in a very short period the Web became commercialised, the whole way of treating the Web changed, and the works were lost in the sea of commerce.

These people weren't interested in the art system and I felt that it was a huge disadvantage that they didn't take part in the general discourse. Very often when you set aside the technological aspect of the work, you realise the issues they are dealing with often already have a history in art.

Another question was how to present work which was made on the computer essentially for one-to-one experience. Since I was really attracted to the work which was totally posited within the computer, and in how it created its own world, I used at the time the metaphor of the book. A book has a physical presence but the moment you open it you get engaged with the content and the physicality disappears. So I finally decided that I had an overview of the area and that I would form this project. And that's how the show 'Can You Digit?' (1996) came into existence. I will just show a little bit of it.

[Slide] This is the Website that was created by Sawed Brooks for the exhibition [www.postmastersart.com/digit/index.html].

The idea was that I thought I had to introduce the medium because it wasn't exposed at all in New York. So I collected twenty-five works and I wanted to show each of them separately because most of them were interactive and I wanted to give an even chance to each work. I created this ship-like shape from these monitors and on each monitor there was one work. In a practical sense it was also important, because all of these were experimental so they weren't very stable and also I felt that if I put several works on one computer, it wouldn't be fair to the work. This way I could create a stable environment because there was nothing else on the machine but that work. From the technical standpoint at that moment it was quite an undertaking to figure it out for a gallery which used to hang paintings. But I think it came out well and I had very few technical glitches. But on the other hand (which is interesting in the context of the current show at the Whitney museum – 'BitStreams' – the first museum show in New York of interactive work), I still ended up hiring a full-time technical person who helped people and made sure that each work was up and running. (I mention that because it took them over a month to figure it out at the Whitney that it wasn't going to work if they didn't have a full-time technical person.)

[Slides] So these are the images from it. I had these works and they were each given an interface – they needed either a mouse or a keyboard or nothing – and I had a few projections. In the whole show there were only two screensavers. One of the distinctions I was trying to keep was that each work could fit on a floppy, because I thought that was the only way I could make it accessible.

From the very beginning one of our challenges was to integrate digital and Web-based art into the mainstream art discourse. Because we really thought that by ghettoising it or defining it by its medium was detrimental, and I believed that to be compatible and live up to expectation, it has to participate in the discourse. The other challenge was to find those artists whose natural medium was the computer – in the exhibition there were a few who were total naturals, totally self-taught people who really touched no other medium.

The other point which emerged after this experience is that it is not a special challenge to deal with digital art because essentially you have to go through the same process as with any other work. That is, you have to understand the work, the ideas, the intention of the artist and then find a specific way to exhibit it without forcing a curatorial idea on it, but to try to communicate these ideas through the way you exhibit the work. As I said, the gallery is a specific situation: it is not a museum, it is not a non-profit organisation, so we had to figure out how to deal with the medium. And the result of it was that after three shows I realised the period of introduction was over and that I had to go back and represent individual artists. And most of the activity that goes on at the gallery today is that.

The other thing I had to deal with in terms of the role of the gallery was that it forced us to continually revaluate what the gallery does. The role of the space diminished to a large extent and we had to think about what kind of environments, what kind of context, existed in which to exhibit this work, and follow that thought process. The other factor was in dealing with a different kind of artist. This can sometimes sound trivial, but in a practical sense, is very important. Not only were these artists removed from the art world, but also they had a valuable skill. Again, it is probably different here, but in the United States, artists are not supported by the government (or very few of them are). There are very few grants, it is very difficult for artists to live from their artwork. So most artists have day jobs. They have to find ways to support themselves and to exist. Before, artists did menial jobs and made little money because they had no practical skills. But this has changed with the digital artists because they have incredibly valuable skills and so they are incredibly independent. It was sometimes a problem and it manifested itself in different ways. One group of artists we worked with got into the commercial world and became very successful and overburdened with commercial work. There, my main job was to try to keep their focus on their artwork and talk them into continuing to make work. On the other hand, there were artists who rejected the new commercial work and had to find new ways of living. But some of them managed to find a balance: they would work for two or three months a year and make enough money to live the rest of the time and they invested all this time, energy and creativity into their art. At the beginning especially, I spent a lot of time just establishing these relationships and figuring out how we could work together.

[Slides] I want to go through the things we did. One of the disadvantages of the gallery is that there is very little time for reflection. It's great that we have the opportunity to do, on average, fifteen shows a year, but it's a continuous process. In the first show there was an interesting thing in how it was perceived. In the audience there was a clear-cut generational gap. Everybody between thirty and sixty – ninety per cent of the people – would walk in, put their hands behind their back and walk around looking at the computers; they wouldn't even approach them and some just walked out. On the other hand, the younger generation came in and got totally engaged and the set-up you've seen worked perfectly. People were engaged in minutes, and were there for hours against the convention of the gallery where people are supposed to spend only fifteen minutes and then go to the next space. 'Can You Digit?' was a huge success. It was overwhelming. On opening night we had at least two thousand people. It also showed that there was a real need and people were interested.

The next show was a direct response to the experiences of the first show. What was emerging was that there was a problem with a lot of works in that they were temporal. People were obsessed with the changes in hardware and software and they never had the time to concentrate totally on what the work was about because they were so immersed in the ever-changing technology. So that was one issue I saw. The other was in what I call the first generation of media artists – Perry Hoberman, Ken Feingold, Ken Goldberg – all these people who were mostly doing their work in Europe (ZKM) and Japan (ICC) and a few other centres. They objected that all the works were on their own computers and that I had ignored the physicality of it. I disagreed with them but I wanted to address this thing and to see how I could approach it differently. I'm basically a proactive person – I like to set a situation and see how I can control the conditions and I find it is very interesting when people have parameters within which to work.

So I came up with the idea of the 'MacClassics' show (1997, www.postmastersart.com/macclassics). The idea was to deal with the physicality. So I proposed the Mac Classic, which is an icon of the personal computer. I bought a lot of these old computers and invited thirteen artists and gave them one each. They were very early Macs so they had almost no memory, almost no RAM, and I said, 'do something within the parameters of this thing.' And that is how the 'Mac Classics' show came into existence. It was fantastic and people came up with very varied propositions. Some people treated it as an object.

[Slide] This person, for instance, was from one of the MIT labs and one of MIT's interests is in the wearable computer – something that is starting to materialise and we are starting to understand what it could mean – and so they were basically made into backpacks. Some people painted them. Some of the early Macs had no hard drive and were working from an 800k floppy disc and artists did artwork within it. One person was doing one-pixel animations. Jodi did what was the first iteration of their inaccessible computers when they created an operating system that was impossible to crack. Later on, a large version was released on CD. The site is still there for you to see.

At that time I also thought that what we were doing was too technology and medium-focused, so I did a show called 'Password: Ferdydurke...' (1998) which was focused on various manifestations of the image from projection and computer-based works. As I said earlier, we were involved in trying to react to what was going on, and one of the projects was not a show but a Bulletin Board. It was at the time of the bombing of Bosnia and what we proposed was that we opened the gallery and anyone could come in and put up an artwork so long as it was closely related to the war in Bosnia. We created a real bulletin board and I collected many of the e-mails that were being posted on the many lists. One reason I mention it is because this show was the beginning of a great relationship with the artist Jon Klima. [...]

SARAH COOK:

Tamas, sorry to interrupt, but I wanted to ask you to comment on the relationship between the gallery as a commercial entity and how the museums are dealing with new media work. For instance, Majec Wisieneski's piece 'Netomat' is now on view at the Whitney though you had shown an earlier version in the gallery, and I wanted to know if the museum had come to you about that?

TAMAS BANOVICH:

What I wanted to say was that with each exhibition we tried to find ways to deal with the particulars. We had one exhibition, 'Behind the Firewall' (2000) which was a direct response to the last Whitney Biennial where they totally butchered all the digital work. First of all, unprecedentedly, they told the artists that they should lend their work but that they would have no influence over how it would be exhibited. The direct result was that the Entropy8Zuper pair pulled out because they didn't want to deal with this installation issue, and one of their works was one the Whitney wanted to present in the Biennial. What the Whitney did in the end, although they had promised that each artist would have their own space or environment, or at least separate computer, was that they put everything on one computer with a projection, and it didn't work. Then they made this weird decision, which I guess was a result of ignorance, that all these works were open to the network, and what happened was that artists subverted it; they would take their projects down periodically and one put up a protest site. For instance, ®™ark auctioned out their space in the exhibition and any artist who was selected could put in their work and make it accessible. So that was one show which was directly related and I showed various works by those artists.

SARAH COOK:

How have museums responded to you running a commercial gallery of media-based work now that museums are looking to show it? You were telling me earlier this year that the museum curators haven't come to the gallery and that's completely uncharacteristic for how museums usually function.

TAMAS BANOVICH:

Not only did they not come, they ignored it [the gallery] for a very long time. It was a totally disjointed process. It's not a complaint and there is nothing personal, but I found it interesting that for years we were the only people in New York who showed new media consistently and comprehensively. And the curator from the Whitney wouldn't even come to the gallery. There are two shows at the Whitney now – one is 'BitStreams' (by the same curator as the 2000 Whitney Biennial's digital component) and 'Data Dynamics' (which is sort of a good break). This is changing now. The two most interesting developments were first that SFMoMA hired Benjamin Weil as their media curator (founder of 'ada'web' in New York). This happened because David Ross, who was the last Whitney director, moved there. So he is the person who understands this medium and was there from the beginning. And then the Whitney hired an adjunct curator of media arts – Christiane Paul – who also is a very knowledgeable person who was around from the very beginning. So it is changing now. And 'Data Dynamics' (which includes three of the five artists I work with at Postmasters) is very thoughtfully put together. If anything, what we achieved through the years is that we consistently got an incredible amount of press for our activities. And those very people who followed the work would come in and for the first few years would just turn around in the door when they saw a media exhibition; they would just refuse to look at it.

You asked specifically about 'Netomat' (www.netomat. net) and I wanted to talk about that. We had to rethink how we operate and one of my ideas was to depart from the fossilised system of selling art and being supported by selling objects. Commissions and all of those variations are basically not a viable source of income, at least not for us. So one of my ideas, which I have started to talk to artists about, was that I would not just represent their artwork but that I would somehow work with them on commercial projects, since all these people were incredibly skillful and many of their artworks were based on software that had other applications than to drive a particular artwork. I want to try to establish some businesses, which in turn could support our activity and depart from the dependence on the old model. For a while, this was just theory, but two years ago we showed the work 'Netomat' by Majec Wisieneski. It was called a meta-browser or an anti-browser. He wanted to show that the Internet is really something other than what we see through the traditional browser and the metaphor of pages, the movies and the radio. His premise was that this was a new medium, a new technology, it doesn't have its own language but it borrows other metaphors. And he set out first to just show what is there. How it works is that there was a screen with floating images, text and sounds and you could talk to it, you could enter anything you wanted in natural language and it would go out to the Web and search many sites and bring back the multimedia results of it in a moving collage, where every object was coming from somewhere else but it suddenly presented all the content that is on the Web in its own context. So if you put in 'existentialism' you could get everything from literature to a stupid song which has the word existentialism in it, to various images and a vast array of information in its own context. So that was the browser. But the underlying technology is an incredible technology which he later expanded to be this whole platform which allows you to speak with this new language of the Internet.

We tried to find a different metaphor for how to present this in the gallery. So we didn't make an exhibition; we made a launch of the software. The day we put it on the Web and made it available for people to download, we at the same time had it in the gallery on several monitors and anyone who came in would have the software introduced to them. It was hugely successful and was downloaded over a million times. Non-art sites and technological sites would put it next to Internet Explorer or Netscape as a proposition for a new browser. So we were thinking that he had already had this idea about this software that would allow anyone to surf and communicate in a different way and take down all these divisions between the Web and e-mail and instant messaging, and just create a new communication language. We concluded that to achieve this, we had to vigorously pursue it and the only metaphor for it was the business metaphor and so we have to approach it as a commercial project. What we want to do is bring out these tools that anyone can use and it is a huge undertaking to create something that is industry strength in terms of software. Within two years we got to the point where we formed a corporation, we raised a seed investment and we formed, with two other partners, a corporation that now exists with six employees, designers and software engineers. This is our art activity at this point. We produce all the art shows and we do commercial projects based on this technology. We will probably release this software by the end of the year. This for me is the first grand experiment to propose something different, a new economic model.

SARAH COOK:

I'm afraid we'll have to stop there. Thank you.

[Audience applause]

MATTHEW GANSALLO

BERYL GRAHAM:

Your next speaker is Matthew Gansallo who was Senior Research Fellow for the Tate Galleries' National Programme. Matthew's knowledge spans architecture and art history, so it's very interesting that he chose to work with some net-artists who got quite a lot of Net coverage, as well as recently and press coverage recently.

MATTHEW GANSALLO:

Thank you very much. I'm going to speak about the encounters I had to overcome while I was commissioning and curating artists for the Tate Website in November of 1999. I studied fine art and have curated some shows with paintings and sculptures; moved on to installation and public art. I also worked in responsive architecture (using light and walls to confuse the users of certain buildings as though they were falling into a well or walking into a wall and so forth). That was one of the remits I had with technology before working as a Senior Research Fellow at the Tate.

Under the aegis of the Tate National Programmes, in November 1999 I was asked to curate and commission art for the newly designed Tate Website and the initial motive for these commissions was to coincide with the opening of Tate Modern in the spring of 2000. Ironically this seminar is taking place now, at a time when Tate Modern is today going to celebrate its first anniversary. The commissions didn't quite make it for the opening of Tate Modern for various reasons. One being that the commissioned artists did not want their works to be swamped by all the press and the glory of Tate Modern and for their works to become a side issue. I will begin by speaking about how I commissioned the artists, and also about the departments at the Tate that helped in the process of curating. When I say they helped, it was in the sense that I had to make them realise that this wasn't a side issue and that they had to take the commissions seriously, with regards to press, development and marketing. A lot of work had to be done in these areas.

The first Tate online projects commission went live with the work of Harwood@Mongrel on the 26th June 2000 and the work of Simon Patterson on the 12th July 2000. My main concern was how these commissions would be perceived as art in the way contemporary art museums like the Tate, define and present art. Another concern was to investigate artists working with Internet technology, with the virtual, that can be presented within the physical spaces of contemporary art museums, without just introducing a couple of PCs and a workstation into a small, stuffy room within a gallery (because that was the initial idea from some quarters). I was also trying to look at viewing the works of different artists that would put a question and perhaps clarification of Web-art, Web-design and art on the Web. I was trying to define those three strands: what is Web-art? What is art on the Web and what are the boundaries we can find between Web graphics and Web art – or Web design graphics and Web-art? I'm not saying that I've come up with any definite answers, but this was one of the starting points for investigation and research for these commissions, which lead us to the ZKM in Karlsruhe in February 2000.

We went to ZKM to look at how these works of a computer and Internet dimension had been curated in a physical space, because we were thinking of doing the work in a similar way to what Julian Stallabrass has done [in 'Art and Money Online'] – putting Net-art in a physical space. But really the remit was 'how do we use the Tate Website to inform and investigate certain artists and artworks?' So there was this idea of having the work strictly online, but the possibilities of also having it in a physical space in Tate Modern or Tate Britain.

I prepared some questions, which I'm going to read out, so that by the time we look at the work you will probably be able to tell me if these questions have been addressed:

– How can Web-artists raise the profile of the autonomous artistic project vis-a-vis heavily marketed entertainment products and are there any examples?
– What forms of synergy can be tapped to create ambitious Web-based art?
– Is it possible to genuinely bring together spheres of e-commerce and the fine art economy to create Web-art? Any examples?
– Has digital art created a particular type of visual dialogue among users on the Net?
– Has this created an art Net-community that can be termed a movement or school?
– In Web-art is it possible to know and recognise the difference between social communication and symbolic representation?
– What are traditional Web-art functions?

– Are there important relations between Web-art and video art and other multi-media forms?

– What is absolutely specific to what makes Web-art a form in its own right?

– How can an environment of ongoing process and human interaction, which has been at the core of the development of artistic projects related to the Internet, be represented and presented in the museum project?

– How do you encourage interaction in both the gallery and online environment?

– Many artists have been interested in the Internet precisely because it has a decentralised power-base and falls outside existing networks of institutions and their legitimising structures. If this is still the case, how does an institution like the Tate take up a role?

Well, it was well worth the trip to [ZKM] and by the time we got back we were all as confused as ever! However, there was one thing I was sure about, which was that this work, whatever form it took, was going to be online. We also looked at work that with a few more applications could sit in the physical gallery or museum space without having too much conflict. So after looking at quite a lot of work on the Web and trying to define which was design and which wasn't (according to what museums say and do) I commissioned two artists because their work was the closest to the rhetoric of viewing and engaging with all sorts of coded symbols to challenge and give insight into different images, conceptions and other issues to do with the production of contemporary art and the history of art. Those two artists were Simon Patterson and Graham Harwood – or Harwood@Mongrel, as he prefers to be called.

Simon Patterson's current work explored the use of colour, perception and language and also his personal reinterpretation of fixed observations of charts and coded information systems. Simon Patterson has never used computers before to inform his work, but his work has a relation to some technological reference and the interfaces of technology. If you know anything about Simon Patterson's work, you probably know the piece 'The Great Bear'(1992), in which he challenged the London tube map by changing all the stations into names of philosophers, actors and other famous figures. When I approached Simon Patterson, I said 'look, what do you think about this? Let's discuss your ideas.' He said he would really like to give it a go and said he believed he was from the school of, 'Oh, I can't touch new media because I've been swamped up by all these galleries and new media is an area that I never ever thought I would go into.' I said, 'well, give it a go and if it goes wrong, don't blame me!'

Then I met with Harwood@Mongrel whose work has really been engaged with computers from the outset and he's also a programer who can make that demarcation between being a programer and creating what we term and what we view as art, in the museum and gallery world. One of Harwood's works is called 'The Rehearsal of Memory' and is in the permanent collection of the Pompidou Centre in Paris. This was one of the works he showed me, which was created using the personalities of the inmates of Ashford Maximum Security Hospital. This work explored, through the use of technology, the peeling off of certain parts of an inmate's body, which revealed their personalities in relation to their convictions. You'd click on an image – maybe a hand or face – and it would peel through and you would hear their voices, what they had done and how they were convicted.

I approached the artists and said 'first, show me your current work,' which we discussed and 'how would you approach creating work for the Tate Website?'

In keeping with what was termed the 'Net-community' and their language, and complementing the contemporary art museum language of criticism within art history, I also commissioned Matthew Fuller, a lecturer, writer and critic of new media to write texts on the emergence of this new type of Net-art and on the completed works of both artists. The title of Harwood@Mongrel's work is 'Uncomfortable Proximity' and the title of Simon Patterson's work is 'La Match de Couleur'. The title of Matthew Fuller's critical text online is: one, an introduction to online art titled 'Art Meet Net – Net Meet Art'; two, 'Bridge the Pieces' for 'Uncomfortable Proximity'; and three, 'The Systematic Arrangement of the Senseless' for 'La Match de Couleur'.

[Slide] Let's see if we can find where they are on the Tate Website. 'Tate Connections – Projects Online'. Hopefully it will come up here.

I will leave it to the audience when viewing the works to judge if the commissions have addressed some of the questions that I presented earlier. But what both artists have done is to recontextualise and recombine the Tate Website, especially the Harwood@Mongrel work, which explores the relationship between new media, Internet art and museum institutions and its traditions. It gives the impression of hacking the Tate Website and keeping with the current concerns of Internet technology, viruses, hacking, etc. Whereby Simon's work takes over the entire screen of the computer, Harwood's work sits behind it and pops up when the computer is being shut down, as a way of asserting its presence.

[Slide] This is 'Uncomfortable Proximity'. It's saying 'Welcome to the Mongrel Tate Website.' If we go into Collections, let's see what happens.

Harwood@Mongrel has taken the Tate Website and rewritten the history of the Tate from a personal point of view. What he did was take a digital camera around Tate Britain after six o'clock when the galleries were shut, photographing the works of J. M. Turner, and made a collage of them and put links in them. Believe me, some curators were not very happy with that, with this chap roaming around the place after hours with a digital camera, while they were about to do some serious work.

Harwood's take on this was that he was linking the history of Tate Britain – in the sense that he was peeling off the fabric and revealing what the Tate used be – with what it has become, as well as mixing it with his family history and his take on how certain institutions have now been converted into institutions of culture (Tate Modern in the Bankside Power Station building, for example). Collating the collection, putting it on the Web and putting it within all the pages of the official Tate Website, so that the audience will read another history, written by Graham Harwood.

[Slides] I just want to compare this with the 'mongrelised' site, which is now known as Tate-Mongrel. What Mongrel has actually done is to give the impression that he has hacked into the site and confused everybody. The idea is that the art is created in the reading of these pieces, when you read them and find out that it isn't really the Tate's official Website, but something completely different.

[Slide] For the Tate Website, Simon was keen to explore the use of sound, colour and the coded information systems of the Internet. Simon Patterson's work presents colours together with their hexi-decimal equivalent, which are matched with every team that has ever played in the French Football League, with the results being read by Eugene Sacromano of Radio France. You have to click on a colour to start. Simon was also interested in the waiting and the expectation of the computer and the Internet: when you click on something and you wait for something to come up. So it started with this series of colour shots. It will slowly begin to change and will make an announcement to each colour of the football league [Website plays]. Just a point to mention, when I click on this it does not go back to the Home Page and this was the initial intention of Simon's work, in the sense that he wanted to trap you here and so you have to go through all the colour charts before you can escape. So

Simon's work and this idea of trapping the viewer and getting into the maze of colours, came about through various meetings with the artist.

I will speak about the curatorial process through the departments that had to begin to engage with this work as an exhibition in itself, rather than just something that was happening on the Tate Web with computers.

As the commissions were going ahead I had to have a lot of meetings with different departments to enable the curating of the work – and I think that's where the 'curating' lay in doing this work, doing it strictly online. The marketing department is in effect the manager of the Tate Website, and since a lot of information and marketing is done through its Website, you can understand the amount of problems that I caused the marketing manager because of Simon's work, and in particular Harwood's work – because of its controversial angle and the artists' personal take on the Tate history.

The Harwood work was meant to drop in to the Tate Website after every fifth hit to the site, so that after every fifth hit you would get the Mongrel site popping up right in front, confusing whoever is using it, making them say 'what's happening here? Is someone hacking through or what?' They would have to find their way all through the Web to find out this is a work of art, or there would be something that the viewers come across that might say 'This is a work of art', and then they could go back to the real Tate site. The marketing department hit the roof: 'We did not spend all this money and time creating the Tate Website to give information about our exhibitions and collections for you to come and start confusing our guests with every fifth hit seeing just the Mongrel work. It's not going to work!' I said, 'well, let's deal!' and that is where we started.

The marketing staff were very concerned that Mongrel was confusing their work – I can understand their point. They said, 'It is all well and good as a work of art but we don't want our hitters to just hit and disappear because we want to speak about a collection, we want to speak about information on exhibitions and education programmes.' However, Mongrel maintained that the art in his work – this particular work – was made when the hitter was confused by the hacked Tate Website, thinking it is the real one and then figuring out that it was not. For him, that was the interaction and where the art lay. I spoke with Simon who also said that he wanted to trap viewers in the maze of colours, so you can't escape unless you find out what you're doing. Simon also maintained that his art for the Tate Website was to trap the audience in this maze of colour and language and they have to go through everything before they can get out of the site, allowing them to engage with the work.

As I said, the marketing department maintained that this would lose potential customers and it became my job to create a clarity between the work – the art – and the business of marketing. So this had to be carefully managed and, in a way, carefully curated. It had to be carefully managed to create a confusion then a realisation, which was what Harwood's work was about, and the erasure then replacement, which is what Simon Patterson's work was about. A decision had to be made whether to curate a demarcation and clarification of when the art starts and ends, or an interruption of the Tate Website by the works, bearing in mind the needs of the artist and the needs of the audience of the Website. While I was busy discussing this about Harwood's work, Simon then decided that he also wanted his work to drop in at every sixth hit!

From the outset I explained to the Exhibition, the Education and the National Programmes teams that I was commissioning artists to work as if we were actually commissioning artists who were creating physical or object-related work for one of the galleries of the Tate. So the artists have the right to present their ideas and their work without any interference whatsoever from people telling them what art is and what they should and shouldn't do. But in this case, it was relatively different and this is where we all learnt how to create a balance – and that was the curatorial challenge. That is what we're now seeing on the Tate's Arts Project Online.

So instead of the drop-in – after numerous meetings with the artists about how it could feed into the Tate Website, the visual space – it was decided the Mongrel work would prop-up the Tate Website, so when you try to click on it, the Mongrel work pops up. Instead of the trap in the maze of colour, the viewer can escape by a click to the bottom of Simon Patterson's work and return to the Tate Home Page.

So Harwood@Mongrel's work was in effect mongrelised to create that demarcation. If you came onto the site, these little details [Slide: putting the Mongrel tag on top of other visual elements and logos] were some aspects of what we had to discuss between the artists and myself, and this is where the curating lay. There were a certain number of pages that had to be mongrelised and we had to discuss the best possible way to do that. On every single page, everything was a mongrelised version – Supporters, Sponsorship, Corporate Involvement.

There is also, at the Tate, a Development Department, which deals with sponsors. The Development Department was concerned about the names of the sponsors and individuals who support the organisation appearing on the Mongrel/Tate Website, and whether or not they would find it offensive. The Development Department were worried that the controversial nature of the Tate-Mongrel site would not attract new sponsors for future exhibition programmes and might make existing sponsors withdraw their sponsorship of future events and exhibitions. In view of this I had to come up with an idea. So letters had to be written to all the sponsors that appear – The Millennium Project; BT; The Guardian; The Observer and so forth –

asking if they had any objection to their logos appearing on the Tate-Mongrel site, as it does on the Tate home Website. All the companies, organisations and individuals Sandy Nairne and I wrote to said that they did not mind if their logos appeared on the Tate-Mongrel site. However, a few did write back saying they would object if their logos were not included on the Mongrel site! So we thought 'Oh, they are interested in art', so that was quite good.

There was also a question about pay. How much should artists who are commissioned to make works online, through a link, get paid? Will they be doing any work? We [the Tate] have programers who are doing the programing, and they are just creating an idea that we are going to program in – so how much can the artist be paid? That was another interesting conversation. However, I am pleased to say that payments to the artists invited to produce work was in tandem with others supplying work for temporary exhibitions at organisations and national museums like the Tate Gallery. I won't tell you how much though!

Another interesting thing that we had to go through, was that art projects online reviewed the standard contract Tate prepares for artists and raised new issues and laws of copyright. For the first time in many years, Tate contracts with artists had to change to accommodate this type of out-of-line commission. Other issues were addressed such as ownership, acquisition, procurement, collection, archiving and provenance – how do you collect and archive such a work? How long will the work be live on the Tate Web? If the artists have the permission to show the work on another Website, when still on the Tate Website, does this mean that they have a contract for one year? Taking into account the nature of the Internet and its communicative ease and access, all these had to be worked into the contracts for the artists.

So these were the issues I had to encounter in the curatorial process. I am, however, encouraged that the

Tate has taken a bold, positive step in this sector of contemporary art and has, in effect, created a platform for more research, experiments and dialogue in museum curating and presenting new media. We were quite aggressive in advertising these works within the marketing, press and promotions departments because, just to take a question that came up from the audience, we didn't want the artists to say that artworks were going out that no one knew about. In the museum context, there are still quite a lot of questions about how new media art is promoted. How does it get marketed and how do people get to know about it? That's still a very fuzzy area for a lot art critics and museum press professionals. How on earth do we begin to write about it and write PR stuff that will get people interested? The fact is that a lot of these departments do not consider this a form of art, so the most important thing is to understand that it is not just about the curating, but it is also about the business of publicising this work and getting the right press, the right critical language, the right critical dialogue and then developing it.

Contemporary art museums of the future will exhibit the virtual and the real alongside one another, crossing and overlapping each other's boundaries, creating an amazing visual and interactive experience within and without walls. It is therefore inevitable that museum architecture will have to change to accommodate the ever-growing advance and innovation in technology. I believe this will enhance the way we use, view and live with new media as part of our cultural consumption. Thank you very much.

[Audience applause]

BERYL GRAHAM:

Thank you very much – that was great. I would now like to open it up to questions.

VUK COSIC:

Why exactly don't you want to tell us how much you paid? I'll find out the figure – I want to know why?

MATTHEW GANSALLO:

Yes, well that's part of this hidden rule of organisations like that, that they keep it quiet. So I'll have to leave it at that.

[...]

TAMAS BANOVICH:

You raised a lot of questions and each of them is a separate topic, for example, dealing with intellectual property and the formulation of all these different relation-ships. I think it's an incredible opportunity that is standing in front of the museum. The museum has a structure: it has sponsors, members and so forth. This can be repli-cated on a much larger scale with the same technology, by using the Internet. If for example, you started an e-mail list. I'm going to say very basic things: it's a great opportu-nity to engage people who come to this site, give them the opportunity to leave their e-mail address and give them a space where they can express themselves and begin to start a very active community. If you want to justify or elevate this area, the best proof would be that in just three months you could create a much larger audience than you get through the door in the whole year, by just starting a community giving people a platform to express themselves or to initiate discussion. The tools are very simple, from e-mail to mailing lists, bulletin boards, and so forth.

MATTHEW GANSALLO:

We discussed a lot of ideas with the press and publicity department regarding what was the best way to publicise this. At the moment we're not sure if we're going to do another series of commissions – this was an experimental time to look at how this fits into the remit of an organisation like the Tate. The Tate deals with its collections and in the sense of showing these collections it does very few new shows. So this can be viewed as a new show, a temporary exhibition programme. An organisation like the Tate, as I've said, does take time to grapple with new media and new ways of looking at curatorial work. I'm sure we'll get there.

PAMELA WELLS:

I would just like to highlight something that you brought up that I find particularly interesting: the artist and the curator being able to collaborate together to question the presenting of potentially challenging work, especially in large institutions that have potentially cumbersome bureaucracy. I find it interesting that you were able, because the artists were making outrageous demands, to then take that request and say, 'actually, I'd like to challenge the whole format of the way the institution works.' Even if everybody knows the answer is going to be 'no', at least it starts a discussion which otherwise wouldn't have been able to get started. So especially with challenging work that people aren't able to pigeonhole as easily or to say this is how it already is being done. I just think personally, with new media, it's a very interesting position because it allows for that space for artists and curators to collaborate on what the parameters are.

MATTHEW GANSALLO:

I can reflect on that. When I was taking this work on I found that dealing with departments that have not actually grappled with this work is something that has to be carefully managed. A lot of the departments' concerns were actually quite valid. There were comments about the work, ranging from 'this is great' to 'get it off my site', or 'wow, isn't it excellent?' and 'what the hell are you lot playing at?' Which was quite good, I think.

MIRIAM SHARP:

I suppose my initial thought was that it is interesting that the Tate decided to commission work, when actually most of its policies are around acquisition, and I wondered why it wasn't seen to acquire works that would give context to the commissioning of new media work and whether that's part of what the Tate's thinking of doing?

MATTHEW GANSALLO:

Well, I'm not aware that the collections team are looking at this area of collecting, but I can say that there is quite a lot of interest in showing it – not just on the Web, but also working with and curating new media in the future. I think that is something that will begin to spark more interest, more research and I think it will be inevitable that it will also look at issues of collection and archiving.

PETER RIDE:

One of the things that I'm interested in is the role of the audience and the curatorial and organisational process and how it defines its audience and recognises that the existence of the audience is a crucial part of the work. I wanted to follow on from what Tamas was saying, in that I do think there are lots of interesting strategies and some museums present online work for very organisational reasons, possibly as you're suggesting, Miriam, linked to what they own and what they don't own; what they have artistic and curatorial rights to. I think there's a really interesting audience with Harwood's work particularly, which is partly about the people within the Tate. I think it's an astonishingly brave and clever piece for the Tate to have commissioned because it is incredibly critical, because in its text it charges the Tate with being institutionally racist, through its heritage – with the origin, obviously, of the Tate's money and the way in which it denies the existence of race as a subject matter in any of its collections. Also it denies the existence of working class – or what Harwood would describe as 'mongrel people' – within the subject matter of any of the images. That is extraordinarily critical of an organisation's history and its ongoing curatorial practice. There's implicit in there as well some very interesting stuff about Saatchi and the way in which art movements can be bought and then capitalised on by organisations, and that Tate Modern is coming at the crest of a very carefully calculated financial wave to create a new Brit-Art movement. I am speaking as somebody who comes from an outside organisation, so I don't have to be very discreet. I think it's a very canny move for an organisation to be critical and yet, because they then say they are very aware, they don't necessarily have to do that much about the awareness. If you buy in an artist who does issue-based work, are you therefore implying you've taken the ownership of those issues in a very artistically postmodern way? Is it a political way of positioning yourself slightly to the left, when actually you're extraordinary conventional? Okay, I've said quite a lot, but what interests me is that it is an educational piece pointed at people within the Tate and the Tate community, so what is the reaction within the Tate?

MATTHEW GANSALLO:

Yes, there has been an interest and a response to this within the organisation. Extraordinarily, it has been an encouraging one: I don't think a lot of colleagues think it is very critical. Maybe that is about buying into the left to feel you're part of the left, when really you're right wing, I don't know. But everybody is saying this is a work of art. There's never been a time when we thought of it as actually being too controversial for somewhere like the Tate Gallery. Yes, it is speaking about all these issues and all that is going on and that's fine. We can handle that. It's a good work and we want to see more of it. Now, if that is actually going to change anything tomorrow or the next year, I don't know. But I can say that the interest within the organisation has been one of well, if we can use this, if we can begin to look at using this as a platform in order to give a pointer to issues of history and curatorial practice, then that's fine. I think that would be too optimistic to say it's going to create an organisational structural change. It might do, but it hasn't done so yet and I doubt whether it will. More work of this kind has to come out, more critical dialogue has to be created, not only about the issues it raises, but also about the notion of art online, before any organisational structural issues will change. It's a work of art and it doesn't change anything I'm afraid – apart from it being an interesting work by an interesting artist.

HANNAH REDLER:

Coming back to curating and collecting media artworks, I'm delighted by these and I loved them when I saw them. I think it's wonderful to have an artist who has been an artist-developer, artist-programmer, artist-entrepreneur and someone coming from the more mainstream contemporary art world, and I think they are great projects. It's interesting that the contemporary art programme that I commissioned at the Science Museum was a mixture of all media – some sculpture, some painting as well as digital technology works. There was no problem in the Science Museum peoples' minds that all of this was art. The only problem that we had there was that it wasn't science. That's a problem I had with the marketing department as they were marketing the launch for the Wellcome Wing. In terms of collecting the objects, they are supposed to be part of a permanent art collection, which leads to all sorts of different problems to do with the fact that current policy in The Science Museum means that if you accession hardware, you keep it in perpetuity for the nation. Therefore if a part breaks, it can't be replaced. So at the moment the Science Museum policy doesn't allow us to collect the content and that is a whole can of worms which has been looked into because the hardware and software are mutable and changing all the time and I think this is making us all begin to think, 'is collecting a particularly good idea?' Curating and allowing research and development is a good idea and I think it comes back to what Tamas said, the museums and institutions actually have to change in response to this. The old way doesn't work.

VUK COSIC:

Can I ask you something? I make Websites for a living – that's my day job. I design information architectures for corporations in the grand economy of Slovenia. When I want to hide or totally remove some stuff in the Website that still has to be there, but I really don't want anyone to see it, first I remove the link from the top level page, then I remove it from the secondary level link lists or navigation tools, and if it is at all possible, I give it another label so it doesn't look like the right thing in a third level. Okay? Now that is exactly how these grand commissions are situated within the Tate Website. It is like – what's the metaphor? – there's this rug and you're putting things under the rug? Now, like you said, you're not on a permanent salary, this project was in part to see what happens. But still, are you in any communication with people who are running the Website? Does the continued functioning of the Website have anything to do with the continuous functioning of those works? That's one question. The other would be whether these two works do anything other than just exist? Are they static, stand-alone entities in cyberspace or are they supposed to mutate, to change? The third thing is just a little confrontation in response to what Tamas had to say: of course the museum will never install a mailing list because yes, they will get an audience, but of the wrong kind! They will get people who are curious, who want answers, who want to talk. They don't want such people. This is a broadcast medium and that's an essential problem that Tate has with the idea of commissioning online stuff, if you ask me.

MATTHEW GANSALLO:

Those are three good questions. The answer to the first one being yes, when this was first commissioned and when it went live, there was about a month whereby nothing happened and I really had to go to the press and the marketing departments' managers and say there has to be a more rigorous campaign for these works. Then I would say in all fairness to them, there were some TV interviews organised and a press release that was sent out and after encouraging them to take this as two new commissioned works which were important, a lot of things were done. But the problem with that, as we mentioned earlier, was that a lot of the critics and journalists, the people who write about art, were not interested and didn't know how to deal with it, I think.

As I said, I was doing something else when I was invited to look at this. It was initially just an experimental piece to see what happened. I think a curator within the Collections Department might be asked to come and do some research in this area and then go back and curate Stanley Spencer or William Blake or whatever. That might be the situation in the future, I don't know. Regarding the third question: has the work done anything, or is it just there? In the first few months we believe that it did generate interest in the sense of, 'oh, well, it's a very critical piece the Tate is doing', or 'great, the Tate has a lot of kudos to be able to do this.' But now, the interest has died down and what I'm looking at is the nature of this type of work within the Web. It has to be reviewed because it is coming up to the one year term of the contract so that by the next contract we will have learned quite a lot from this. It is something that has to be constantly there and that is what I hope the powers that be will be able to push forward.

PETER RIDE:

While we are talking about big institutions, I think it's worth saying some sorts of organisations have a particular behavioural pattern and it seems to me that really large organisations like Tate Gallery and the Science Museum, just by their very nature (they call themselves and think of themselves as national institutions) are huge, and they move like the National Health Service or the Civil Service body – it takes them ages! They have this historic trajectory where the small things going on are the singular art projects and they are always absorbed by a much bigger pattern and they need to know what's happening six months in advance, and they are not flexible within that. It's little pockets within those larger organisations that do the really interesting stuff and sometimes they don't know what one an other does. I think that one of the people who is doing really interesting work at the moment is Honor Harger at Tate Modern, and the Web-casting and dialogue that she has set up with online communities. But to me, one of the most interesting things about this is the question: can you easily commission, develop, curate works that are about flexibility and risk-taking if you become a large organisation? This is a question for the BALTIC also, and other organisations like that. Or to Eddie Berg about organisations like Video-Positive, which has a reputation for doing very innovative, fast-on-their-feet work. Festivals can easily and rapidly construct a context around work as can small art organisations or agencies like DA2 which aren't a building. But a big organisation, whose identity is so massive, and who see themselves as being a repository of authority – it's very hard for them to be flexible.

VUK COSIC:

It's not a building that we're talking about – it's a bunch of humans you can talk to, and they're able to understand stuff and I think that understanding might just be a first step. We're talking about the understanding of things, not so much their tragic lack of velocity.

TAMAS BANOVICH:

I wanted to say that new media has an incredible chance because you can subvert these systems and run around them in circles and therefore force them to be interested. In the States they really go after these things and for a couple of years there will be a very high profile for that issue and every museum now hires a media curator because they are forced to, because they are subverted into it. Through the Web, people manage to create a huge public interest.

SARAH COOK:

One of the things I remember Vuk saying at another conference was that artists are the ones who are moving faster and they're the ones who are continuously changing their projects and museums should – and this is true for us here at BALTIC when we're dealing with commission-ing – be keeping apace with the artists rather than trying to keep apace with or being weighed down by, the build-ing.

[Audience applause]

DAY ONE CONCLUSIONS/DISCUSSION

BERYL GRAHAM:

We have a short list of issues which we think have come up during the day and we need to find out from you whether we're not covering key issues that have come up from your own experiences, which we should be talking about as new media curators and artists.

HANNAH REDLER:

We seem to be talking only about Internet art and I'm wondering if the group here is interested in interactive and new media installations as well? I'm very struck by the fact that the Tate is getting such a high profile here, given that it was just last year that they commissioned the two Web works and produced the show on now, all of which I greatly admire. But I think it is telling that the Tate is only committing to Internet work which is a bit more low-risk. I also have to say that the National Museum of Science and Industry and the National Museum of Photography in 1999 opened the first gallery in the UK that has committed permanent work by artists, such as Jeffrey Shaw, Paul Sermon, and Jane Prophet. This isn't known about. We present the Tate here but we don't present that because that's not the real art world. I think it is wonderful that the Tate is doing this but we need to understand that this isn't just a contemporary art situation. The National Museum of Photography is also a sister museum of the Science Museum in London which has two works by Christian Mueller, one work by Tessa Elliot, one by Jones Morris and one by David Rokeby – they opened last year with the Wellcome wing. As the curator, I am absolutely disgusted that so few people know about it because the artists put in a lot of effort and expected to get quite a high profile from a national museum. So I'm not just having a dig at the Tate or the art world but more at the pigeonholing in the lines of communication and how this sort of work is promoted. That is the issue.

TAMAS BANOVICH:

I see a huge role for the institutions and it is going in that direction. It seems it just needs a mental break, and perhaps the Tate has already taken that, to assign to it as much importance as to any other project. Then I think following the logic, there are many ways for institutions to be involved – from commissioning new work, to maintaining sites, to archiving.

SARAH COOK:

I can respond to Hannah's point by saying that the previous BALTIC seminars have obviously been about looking at other models of production as well, though we are in the position of commissioning; we are developing a factory that is going to be commissioning new work continually and having artists-in-residence. I think that Julian Stallabrass' show, and also what Matthew has talked about regarding the Tate, is related to BALTIC's programming in so far as they have been commissioning, building on already existent programming, trying to figure out ways in which it fits into the space. I'm excited to hear about these permanent installations you mention and I'm glad that the participants at the seminar represent this range of interests and projects. The issues are the same, whether it is developing new software and trying to figure out how to get it out into the world, or providing new opportunities for artists: how do you start a commission and where do you take it from there? What is the lifespan of some of these projects?

PETER RIDE:

What really amazes me is what Tamas was saying, that none of the curators actually came around to the gallery. One of the things that seems inherent to new media practice is that it crosses over so much and it seems that people are always cross-referencing each other: discussion lists are very animated; people are communicating regularly, contributing to lists such as Rhizome; people in the US are aware of what is happening in the UK, people in the UK are aware of what is happening in the States. There is such an interesting crossover that it surprises me that things don't filter up.

CHRIS BYRNE:

I think we've been here before. This is one of my bugbears. If we're talking about the Tate specifically, then we should remember it took them a long time to accept video art as a practice as well, and it has something to do with the relationship of media art to the art world or the art market, and levels of acceptance of certain kinds of practice. It was rare for video art, apart from video installation, to be show in Tate Britain (as it is now) until relatively recently, say the early 90s, although the practice had been going for some time before that. Maybe the catch-up time has been less in terms of Internet practice but perhaps there is a similar phenomenon now that it has crossed into certain mainstream perceptions in the art world. Therefore institutions can step in and show this type of work because it is deemed to be of interest.

JULIAN STALLABRASS:

I'd like to reinforce that point and add to it: you could say the same thing about photography, which was just not considered an art form at all at one time. At least the lag time is getting shorter, which is perhaps encouraging.

VUK COSIC:

Julian, photography was not about a reference to the art system, as much as Net art is about the art system, so what happened was that most of the Net artists retired as soon as the system tried to incorporate the work in their arenas – so I think that is new. Plus all Net art is being curated by old video art curators such as Barbara London and John Hanhardt.

The expression or word 'net.art' came about because we were anxious to give ourselves a classification or label before anyone else from the art bureaucracy came to give us one. This expression 'classics of net.art' was a joke about the way the museums wanted to talk to us and put us in a group so that they could deal with us. So I did a project called 'A History of Art for Airports.' It was all done in a humorous fashion, so people wouldn't have to think too much, or at least if they did have to, they didn't have to take it seriously. But it was part of the work itself to think of the ways it could be incorporated into some larger net. It is better for you to find a place there than to wait for the person who has never been in your shoes to find a place for you.

NINA CZEGLEDY:

I'd just like to say a word about classifications. We've talked mostly about Net-based art today, but if we talk about new media there is also the CD – what do we do about showing and presenting and creating audiences for CD-based work? What about embodied interactive work? What about certain types of robotics? These all fit into our area.

HANNAH REDLER:

Are we taking it as a given that we have to differentiate media art from art? One of the problems I have found is that people who don't understand technology often don't know where the art lies and so they don't know what they're looking for. This is a particular problem with work where it is artists working conceptually with software, or innovating something where the code is very exciting but it doesn't necessarily translate in the final experience.

CHRIS BYRNE:

I had a narrower point about the relationships between curating in developmental agencies and institutions, galleries, museums. This might be a talking point specifically for the UK because of agencies like Film and Video Umbrella and DA2 and other models, which are not based in physical buildings. It might be interesting to talk about the dialogue between those types of organisations and physical (land-based) spaces.

BERYL GRAHAM:

The shortlist of things that have come up for me have been:
1. The concepts of lag, which I thought was very interesting. Tamas said that 'the period of introduction is over', which I think it is for some people, especially if you're

within the media art world, but I still think for other people there is some need for instruction and that very much depends on audience.

2. Audience. Tamas again mentioned a very rough and ready judgement – those from thirty to sixty had one reaction and those below that had another reaction. A lot of the feedback about audience is very anecdotal, which I think is useful, but beyond that we really have very little evidence on which to base our new relationships with audiences, if they do exist.

3. We've talked a little bit about aesthetics and how to show this stuff. Quite often this has worked in metaphors – is it like an office, is it like a home, should it only be shown at home? What if you don't use the Internet at home?

4. Also the idea of categories. Categories of curators – whose department does this go in? Whose departments are you working with (which could range from marketing to video)? If you're buying in curators, is that like starting a new department or do they just work with existing curators? Are there categories of new media art, and are they dividing into Net-art and 'other'? In which case 'other' might be the more physical stuff and may include the first generation of new media artists as Tamas described them (Perry Hoberman, for example, and those who did mostly physical installations).

TAMAS BANOVICH:

I think the education process is never over. But one important thing is that generally I think a deeper understanding of the medium would make all those questions much easier to answer. I think it would be interesting to organise forums where people who make media art would explain the medium. That would answer a lot of questions right away.

SARAH COOK:

From this afternoon I think we have learned a lot that we can put towards our thinking about how BALTIC might develop. These seminars are a learning experience for this new institution. I think that as we have many artists speaking tomorrow who are working on new commissions, we might come back to issues of real-space location and place.

ILIYANA NEDKOVA,
'Consolations for Curatorial Inadequancy'*

BERYL GRAHAM:

I would like to introduce Iliyana Nedkova. Iliyana is currently Associate Curator at FACT [Foundation for Art and Creative Technology] and is also doing a PhD concerning the curatorial theory and practice of new media. She is based between Liverpool and Sofia in Bulgaria and has been collaborating with Nina Czegledy on a project called 'Crossing Over', which is an annual micro-festival of digital film culture. I will let Iliyana introduce the theme of her talk this morning, which I think is a very apt one.

ILIYANA NEDKOVA:

Thank you very much Beryl. I would like to pick it up where we left it yesterday and also extend a bit on what Matthew and Tamas referred to as the challenges of new media curatorship. I have brought with me some anecdotal

*Homage to Alain de Botton ('Consolations of Philosophy', Penguin Books, 2000)

evidence and some speculations arising from my current curatorial philosophy and practice. I would like to suggest some scenarios for coping with what could be called 'curatorial inadequacy', and indeed offer some consolations for curatorial inadequacies. I'll just use some points of web reference in the background; [Slide] here is a bit of the first web reference called 'www.cult.bg', where 'bg' stands for Bulgaria.

If you happen to be a new media curator in Bulgaria then it's more than likely that you will be suffering from a form of identity crisis, fuelled by a sense of cultural inadequacy. It's because 'new media curator' is still a very dodgy title across Bulgaria for at least two reasons. The root structure of curate – or curator – has a certain explicit sexual connotation and you're more likely to experience bits of one's title – 'New Media Curator' – scribbled graffiti-style in obscure public spaces or used in a cocktail of fruity street language. But also in the Bulgarian mentality, the foreign language borrowing 'media' derives from the term 'mass media' – indicating manipulative, ideologically driven and ideologically biased culture. What is more, 'media' is related to 'multi-media', wherein 'multi' stands for an offshoot of 'a Multi-Group' – a group of corrupted companies run by the local mafia, which refer to their businesses as 'Multi-art', 'Multi-club' or Multi-whatever.

Despite this linguistic insecurity a new breed of Bulgarian new media curator operating from within the country or outside the country has emerged. For the last ten years we have collectively been trying to confront this peculiarly constructed public opinion and attitude and pave the ground for a more adequate and well-informed reception of new media works, as well as for a new audience engagement with some fine examples of curatorial or artistic practice.

But as many new aspects of new media culture remain undefined as yet, not least the identity, role and function of the curator – the new media curator – in Bulgaria and perhaps, by and large, beyond Bulgaria, I wondered how we, as poorly misunderstood and curatorially inadequate souls, can possibly find consolation in this absence of a public lexicon, at a time when new media art is going through an identity crisis itself? In this presentation I would like to suggest that a possible consolation for curatorial inadequacy in this unarguably unfocussed art world – the new media art world – is firstly curating and creating across borders, and secondly the advantages of doing this with friends. So let's talk about borders.

It may help the curatorially inadequate to have spent some time journeying and conferencing around Europe and beyond. By travelling across/between/within different frontiers by any means of communication – be it on horse-back or by Easy-Jet, or just in the imagination – be it over a book or the Internet, we are invited to exchange our local prejudices and the self-divisions they have induced for less constraining identities as citizens of the world. We will hopefully be able to follow in the footsteps of the ancient philosopher Socrates who, when asked where he came from, didn't say 'from Athens', he just said 'from the world.' The world, and the new media world in particular, has recently revealed itself as a far more peculiar world than anyone had ever expected. What is deemed as peculiar and what counts as normal seems to be at the core of this inadequacy debate. It is the world of peculiarities, rather than abnormalities, that fits into the logic of new media, and this is what Lev Manovich and possibly Manuel Costells, cultural theorists both, have revealed in the post-industrial Net age we live in: there is an unprecedented rise of the network society whereby personal variability and individual peculiarity are the norm. New media art and technology are all working to convince us that we're all different and that our choices and desires are all very unique. [Slide] Just a bit of distraction: this is the portal for ultra-contemporary Bulgarian culture (www.cult.bg). I will just leave you with a bit of clear sky here.

New media has been doing this, as if to compensate for the old media corresponding to the industrial and the mass consumption of society feeding on the same goods and beliefs. It is old media that produced millions of copies – almost Hollywood-like media factories – and distributed them to all citizens via mass distribution channels like print, broadcast and cinema. Now in the early years of the new century, both fascinated and facilitated by the world of new media art, we are on our way to offering every citizen the opportunity to construct their own customised style and select an ideology from a large number of choices. And hereby Lev Manovich would rightly enquire: "are we on the way to constructing a new utopia of a perfect, networked society, composed of unique individuals?"[1]

I wonder, are these the very same new individuals of the Net-age for whom new media art initiatives such as as www.canalweb.de or www.superchannel.org are designed, as if to provide a mere consolation through their very custom-tailored, specialist services? [Slide] www.canalweb.de can perhaps be best described in terms of old media – a cross-over between an interest print magazine and live TV talk show. Except that it is site-specific – it's all in German by the way as you've already gathered – so it is really designed for this site-specific audience who is very well dispersed across the Internet channels. So the curators at www.canalweb.de are, as a matter of fact, commercially-driven producers and service providers, outsourcing their editorial responsibility to the experts within any group of self-identified users, ranging from chess players to people living with AIDS.

[Slide] The approach favoured by www.superchannel. org is entirely different in that its critical slant comes from the gift economy and e-democracy and is focused on

1. His essays can be found at www.manovich.net

providing the actual means and skills of web-casting production to its end users. www.superchannel.org is actually established by the Danish artists collective 'Superflex' and www.superchannel.org is mostly publicly funded and produced by FACT, often guided on the side by FACT-based curators. It often bypasses the entertainment drive of www.canalweb.de, yet again it caters for the specific requirements of its users. Amongst the www.superchannel.org users there are residents of Liverpool tower blocks – a number of whom are in their seventies and eighties and by now, as you can gather, they are leading-edge narrow-casters and web programme presenters. Unsurprisingly, their issue-based programmes, like 'Coronation Court', often dwell upon the glamour and despair of high-rise living and their immediate community's problems.

It is tempting to infer that the state-of-the-art streaming technology lends itself to various curatorial approaches, all interested in the further breakdown of the society into ever-smaller networks and groups. As www.canalweb.de programme director Julienne Shultze pointed out, "we're probably nurturing another utopia here by trying to reach the opinion leaders rather than those millions of people clicking on the site – or 'the clickers' as I would call them." Likewise, www.superchannnel.org curator Maria Brewster, based at FACT, spells out that one of the 'pitfalls' of such a project, which solicits "attention from formerly non-art audiences", can't possibly "bypass overnight the differences between users of established culture and the culture of the art world".

Such a testimony of cross cultural and curatorial practice, of other countries and lifestyles, has helped alleviate the sometimes oppressive atmosphere of my home region, including the still-fledgling new media art scene there. Curating and creating Bulgarian media arts and culture at the edge of the twenty-first century is more of an ambitious and unfinished research project. I have been conducting this project from the curatorial perspective of a part-time insider commuting between cultures and cities. My curatorial practice, as that of some fellow curators, has been a classic tale of migrating and merging identities. It's a tale of two cities – navigating and negotiating the differences and the cultural and geographical distances between Liverpool and Sofia in my case, or Sydney and Sofia in Antoanetta Ivanova's case; Montreal and Sofia in Biliana Velkova's; Basel and Plovdiv in Albena Mihaylova-Stüssi's; Chicago and Sofia in Zhivka Valyavicharska's and the list goes on. So, knowing the old and new media arts from and beyond Bulgaria inside out is not just my ongoing project. I'm no longer on my own. Back in 1995 when I started pursuing curatorship and joined the lonely, long distance run of self-development, I felt the absence of others – but no longer, which is a source of consolation and a great relief.

Now, a few years later it seems as if there's been a steady need for 'curators on demand' – soon to be known possibly as 'outsource curators', associate or guest curators. Paradoxically, they are often guests in their own home countries. For example, I very often get asked to guest curate a show in Bulgaria. So no wonder that a whole nomadic community of wandering curators has got two or more cities' tales to tell, not unlike my fellow countrymen or countrywomen. As the new networked society continues to offer displaced, nomadic lifestyles as the preferred choice rather than one economically enforced, it also accelerates its ways of processing more and more data – as if being greedy for more resolution, more bandwidth and more everything (which streaming technology is a very good example of).

So the good news, I suppose, is there will be an increasing need for outsource curators for interfaces, as Steve Dietz would put it. They will be the reincarnated curators of the network age, filtering through the sea of data. We, however, need to know our trade well, advancing our filtering, swimming and surfing skills, for there is another sea to swim through and this is the sea of ultra-prosperity, the richest of the super-rich. This is the sea of the roaring zeros whereby the new BMW status symbol will allegedly be philanthropy and the personal charitable foundation. Ultra-prosperity is expected to be churning out millions of dollars or pounds and millions of ideas, but it will be chronically short of managerial skills to make use of those millions. Ultra-millionaires don't have the skills – but 'ultra-curators' do – or they had better acquire them now.

Yet, while waiting for ultra-prosperity to dawn upon us, as it has apparently done in a certain valley across the pond, we are still trying to cope with mountains of cultural inadequacy. Interestingly, what has helped in combating the state of anxiety and curatorial inadequacy caused by the belated arrival of Bulgaria into the media art world – this sense of time-lag we touched upon yesterday – has been part of my 'conspiracy' or 'missionary project' to provide opportunities for cultural tourism for Bulgarian and by and large, Eastern European artists and mediators.

Net-based travel and tourism seems to be taking off now. But once upon a time the vicarious, Net-based travel had yet to exercise its allure on the new conceptual 'generation.com' of Bulgaria who didn't quite fancy trading their ambitions to travel in real time and real space for sipping their virtual coffee in the digital bistros of Paris. Now, a few years later, most of them have had their tanta-lising cravings to be integrated in viable international projects of media culture satisfied. It was only soon after their touring appetite was saturated, that they went on to settle in Bulgaria. Having been recognised beyond the walls of their neighbourhood, they have started building up local media community centres. Having been recognised beyond the walls of their immediate surroundings, they have started building up the local media community network, while at the same time constructing a previously non-existent new media art infrastructure. To fill in this infrastructural gap, the Institute of Contemporary Art – based in Sofia – has recently teamed up with the largest grant-giving body in town, the Soros Centre for the Arts, to set up the first educational framework for curatorial training. Set up away from the formal educational sector, this first curatorial workshop aimed at shaping the first generation of art managers and converting the classically-trained art historians into ultra-curators.

There are quite a few new independent hubs of sustained media art activity that have emerged and have been eroding the previously media-innocent climate since the mid-nineties, and here are just a few examples. There is a place called 'Interspace' which is a centre for media production and critical debate including the animated database of ultra-contemporary Bulgarian culture, www.cult.bg. There are a number of other newcomers including the association for contemporary art called Art Today, Vision N-Forms Foundation, the Red House, ATA Centre for Contemporary Art or the XXL Gallery for media-related events, as well as the zet-mag and malek e-zines – all shaping the newly-rising media culture of Bulgaria.

However, we are yet to experience any consistent effort on the side of the traditional museum culture across Bulgaria and this is no exception to the rule – Matthew raised this issue yesterday. The traditional museum culture across Bulgaria still needs to catch up on the new media art front by working with in-house or external curators. We should perhaps believe that contemporary artists and inter-faces have much to teach museums about the relevant possibilities of a new medium in a changing society. What is beyond doubt though is that well-travelled artists and curators have proven healthy critics and opponents of regional incomprehension and provincialism. Our province may have many virtues but these don't depend on it being our province, and a foreign land may have many perceived faults, but I wonder, if your customs are unusual, does this make you culturally inadequate? Surely nationality and familiarity, as most of us know, are absurd criteria by which to decide whether something is good or bad.

Neither is gender such a criteria. I'll just go briefly into some gender issues now. One futuristic or speculative aspect to ponder upon is the question of how many women will be using blind-dating technology and what courting techniques will they be employing? What will be at the other side of the ones and zeros for them and how will they sustain their love/hate relationship with the digital art world?

Yet creative technology as we know it today, may not be the final frontier for an increasing number of women curators and artists in and beyond Bulgaria, but they boldly go where no one else has gone before. So, coincidentally or not, Bulgarian culture of the nineties presents itself as run and governed by women artists and practitioners. Women dominate the curatorial network of artists and producers. As a result, creative technology is recognised as a very elegant occupation that readily includes – indeed welcomes – outbursts of intimacy and humour, or the fires of urgency and immediacy. There is not just this love of experimenting, but there is a lust for blind-dating technology. Indeed, this peculiar rise of the network society of women has prompted me to curate – remotely – my first women-only Net-based show and this is the only work of mine that I will briefly take you through.

[Slide] In search of giddy romance or true – but always blind – love, six women artists at the forefront of the generation.bg have come together to tell their own blind-dating stories at www.blinddata.net. The project 'Blind-dating Technology 2000' was in fact produced with no budget and premiered at Mediaterra 2000 for their second international art and technology festival and symposium, and exhibited at the Factory, in the Athens School of Fine Arts in November 2000.

Expressed with a dizzying potion of love, excitement and critique, these are six tales, which you can explore further at your leisure through the six gateways on the website. These are tales of unrequited passion and seduction of the new digital partners, tales of the ones and zeros of digital romance. Each rendezvous with Mr. PC – politically correct or personal computer, you decide – inspects the neo-techno language used for authoring in the Internet environment.

[Slide] Just as an appetiser – you can arrange your blind date or blind-data at your leisure at any time afterwards – I would like to take you through two of the six works. Here is the Cover Story. This is the title of an artist's work by Zornitsa Sofia, one of the rising stars of new media art in Bulgaria. In her Cover Story the HTML innocent cover girl goes out on her first blind date at the Marihuana Café, Backstage nightclub and ends up in bed with Mr. PC. [Video plays] It's very literal, yet stylish. Interestingly, the tragicomic comments voiced over the basic animated imagery expose the underlying hi-tech aspirations of the women in love.

What was really striking for me through this curatorial process was that the ethos of the blind-dating technology was predicated on gross uncertainties from the start, allowing the sense of curatorial inadequacy to creep in. The experience of remote online co-control shared with six artists and complimented by an odd troubleshooting phone call from afar, was far from rewarding and often just on the edge for me.

For a start, techno-terror reigned havoc in the backspace of the project web-zone. The two browsers Internet Explorer and Netscape Navigator were still waging their star wars over the project's fonts and font sizes while we were constructing it. Then, the land telephone line at the designer's home studio – who was one of the artists in Sofia – had gone missing and with it her dial-up access to the demo website. A cable man was called in as a matter or urgency to rescue the project and to reinstall the underground telephone cable. Apparently the shadow Bulgarian economy, which thrives on the recycling of the copper wire from the stolen telephone cables, had traumatised the micro-climate of this blind date. On top of it all, the server in Athens had gone down, when it was much needed to be up. The ftp transfer had experienced an unprecedented slowdown. As if this was not enough, hackers had surfaced as if from nowhere – well, you can expect this from Sofia as the capital city of hackers – while the designer worked away from home at the nearest Internet Café in town. I was working away from home as well, busy curating another project at the Wexner Centre for the Arts in Columbus, Ohio. What is more, the artist assigned with the role of showing and telling the festival crowd all about the site, on-site, at the gallery premises in Athens, had gone through fire and hell to get her visa issued, only to find out that she was refused visa entry into neighbouring Greece for no good reason. Meanwhile, the Athens festival curators on-site had employed very elaborate installation design tactics which had successfully absorbed the artists' and curator's fees and reportedly killed the intimate artistic gestures of the blind-dating technology project.

Once again, the tension between the big and the bit-screen experience of new media work – we talked about that yesterday, though we've not resolved it – has surfaced again in this blind-dating technology project, possibly echoing Beryl's questions: how do we show new media art to people? How do artists ensure it gets to be seen as it should be? Is it with big dark rooms or comfortable, squashy lounges? Computers on desks or purely online? I have also wondered, what do we want to escape from, if anything, or what do we want to compensate for through the bit-screen experience? As we know, the big screen experience with its periodic trips to the dark, relaxation chambers of the movie theatres, became a routine survival technique for the citizens of the industrial era. I wonder what we're searching for now through the bit-screen experience? Consolation for what?

At least two curatorial survival scenarios have emerged out of these busy records of peculiar incidents: firstly, the urge to view 'Blind-Dating Technology 2000' as a pilot, non-fixed project with a potential to be developed further, an urge corresponding to the most prominent of the principles of new media art – variability. So be on the lookout for 'Blind-Dating Technology 2001, version 2.0'.

The other consolation for this instance of curatorial inadequacy, which on reflection was partly due to curatorial over-booking and excessive trust in the power of remote e-communication, is possibly friendship. Friendship can bring consolation for accusations of abnormality, usually manifested in the slightly alarmed question: 'really, how weird?!' This is normally accompanied by a raised eyebrow, implying the denial of legitimacy or humanity – bits of which I had encountered in Athens when one of the artists was granted no visa. In its extreme form, this denial leads to cultural misunderstandings. In our case, it led to the misdirecting of the exhibition funding towards a grand scale, big-screen installation, rather than to the artists in the first place.

This is where friendship comes into the picture – a friend being among other things, someone kind enough to consider more of us as normal than most people do. We may share judgments with friends that in ordinary company would be censored as too weird, too sexual, too despairing, too clever or too vulnerable. Yes, friendship is a minor conspiracy against what other people think of as reasonable. I would argue that friendship is an essential component of healthy and adequate curatorial policy. It was because of long-standing or recently-earned friendships with artists that the 'Blind-Dating Technology' project managed to survive the difficulties and has manifested itself with a bit of dignity. It has done so, while, quite ironically, addressing different romantic and aggressive aspects of communication, exposing the very subtle mechanisms of human and computer relationships, aiming to make them more explicit, suggestive and great fun to indulge in.

I am tempted to leave you here with just a few thoughts. How many of the new media curatorial co-productions known to us today are run on the engine of friendship and how will that implicate on the project's data and interface (in other words – form and content) in the long run? How could the new media museum wear the sign 'partners and friends wanted' with dignity to avoid its own curatorial inadequacies also beyond the art world? How could the curators ensure that the artist-led community projects now proliferating in the new media sector, are being sensitive and morally responsible to the particular community or partner's needs? How could we possibly maintain the precarious balance between being very pro-active and responsive through process-led projects whereby the product comes second, yet, nonetheless is of equal importance? Borrowing Steve Dietz's observant remark, how could curators who once used to be playing "sage on the stage", now enjoy their new fallen-from-grace status of "guides on the side"[1], or else being kind and considerate friends? With institutions focused on outreach, to an extent that collaborative practice and open-source channels are desirable – and the Internet is just being a great facilitator in the process – the curator's role is to make media art communicable, mediative and manageable. I think we should probably all agree here.

Again, is this to be done by being led by the art and the artists (as Beryl Graham pointed out on the CRUMB list once, or possibly more than once)? Perhaps the final point (and it is really the final point here for me) in advocating the need for friendships, for collaborative models, for alliances within the new media art world, is posing the

1. Steve Dietz's website can be found at www.walkerart.org/gallery9/dietz

question, 'if the content or the data is king, who is the emperor?' Is it the form or is it the audience? Is it the interface or is it the user? And despite the semantic inadequacy of this power-corrupted metaphor, we are perhaps moving towards the healthy convergence and swapping of roles and relationships between artists, curators and audiences.

And yet, if we were not to be blessed with friendships every time we curate a project, perhaps there is a consolation for that too. Perhaps we can discover another fine form of compensation called 'authorship' or 'writing'. As one of my favourite writers Alain de Botton, argues in his book 'Consolations of Philosophy', when he talks about Michel de Montaigne as one of the finest minds in the history of philosophy, Montaigne might have begun writing his book of essays to alleviate his sense of personal loss. Botton writes that Montaigne's writings – collected in his Essays and published some time in the 1580s – may serve in a small way to alleviate our own sense of loss and inadequacy. In de Botton's words:

"Montaigne became himself on the page, as he had been in the company of his friends. Authorship was prompted by disappointment with those in the vicinity, yet it was infused with the hope that someone else out there would understand. His book of essays is an address to everyone and no one in particular. He is aware of expressing his deepest thoughts to strangers in bookshops and yet, we should be grateful for this paradox – booksellers are the perfect destination for the lonely."

You have to wonder then, given the number of books that have been written, is it because authors, including new media curators, couldn't find anyone to talk to?

Thank you very much.

[Audience applause]

HANNAH REDLER:

I was really interested in the point you raised about the www.superchannel.org and www.canalweb.de projects, to do with the art world and the community's needs and I wondered if you could say a little more about that?

ILIYANA NEDKOVA:

Yes, well in researching my topic for today, I was really struck by this comparative analysis between Superchannel.org and Canalweb.de, who are apparently pursuing the same sort of goals, but they are going about it in totally different ways. Superchannel.org is one of the ongoing projects that has been nurtured at FACT for about eighteen months now. It actually comes from the frustration that streaming technology or Internet-based activities are not there to be misused or indulged in just by a number of – very privileged – people but they can probably do something for and give some hands-on experience to, a very particular set of people that we've approached through creating lots of partnerships, city-wide in Liverpool. And this is a very particular set of residents, in Coronation Court, which is Liverpool's oldest tower block. It really was a very good way of saying, 'look, you've now got the means and ends of production and possibly the dissemination, so what would you like to talk about between yourselves?' So this was a very good chance to empower, by saying that this technology is there for more democratic purposes than you would imagine. You can certainly browse through and see what the particular needs and demands of this very tangible community of new users are. I guess Claire Doherty and Eddie Berg who are here with us, can probably tell you a bit more about it – this particular process of working with these seventy year olds. They are exciting people.

BERYL GRAHAM:

I have a question. I loved your phrase about outsourced curators. Yesterday we were talking about this with Matthew Gansallo and how his status as a slight outsider – as a guest – did enable him to do things which maybe resident curators couldn't have done, by talking to various departments and by forging new relationships with those various partners. But outsourcing is traditionally a way of stripping the rights from workers. So I just wondered if you could say a little bit more about this? How powerful did it feel being the guest?

ILIYANA NEDKOVA:

I think there are two issues at stake here. First of all, this is a borrowing from the e-commerce world. They love talking about the 'outsource expertise' that they would bring in, and that's what would drive the e-economy, because quite frankly, it's less expensive, it's much neater to work in this way. Increasingly the art world is mimicking the business world. I wondered whether that might be a matter of phraseology or just a very well-justified need for us as curators to be more flexible, to work in this kind of environment and not necessarily to expect that a big organisation like Tate Modern would have the same ethos, profile or agenda as a smaller organisation and would necessarily have the position reserved for an in-house curator. There are definitely various models to be applied here and we have to be really careful when we are raising our expectations too high in terms of what an organisation should look like in terms of treating its staff and external outsource members.

KAREN ALEXANDER:

Could I just add to that the idea of the friendship lines in relation to outsourcing, because I think, again, the issue around outsourcing is about who people know and trust in relation to that. But at the same time, the friendship lines that exist within networks are really important and the question is, whether those networks can be used to inform institutions?

ILIYANA NEDKOVA:

Very much so and I think even the European bureaucrats wouldn't shy away from this particular line of thinking. Interestingly, one of their guidelines advises you to get to know your European project partners first. If we read between the lines of the European Commission guidelines, knowing your cross-border partners is just a step away from making friends. So I think we're being very timid here, not to confess to this. We have to be really honest that this is what drives curatorial practice. We all need to make our own little alliances in order to manage and deliver a project, and we're also trying to put all sorts of grandiose titles to something that may be just another instance of extended friendship.

KAREN ALEXANDER:

I think what is useful is to make that explicit, but at the same time, as soon as that becomes explicit it is to understand the problematic in it. That's why I think it is very important.

PETER RIDE:

I think that issue about collaborative working across different boundaries is a really complex and interesting one, and I would be really interested to see if a Commission ever put in its recommendations, formally, 'work with friends'. But I completely understand that in this sense they could certainly advocate 'you should, if you're setting up networks, work with people whose working patterns you understand.' But the way you started off was very interesting, talking about there being a particular cultural context in a place like Sofia and what curating means there. A notion of curatorial practice might be completely different in Ohio, Sofia, Sydney or wherever, and yet you're working with different groups simultaneously – how do you then discover and negotiate how they understand what curatorial practice is and what they want from you?

ILIYANA NEDKOVA:

Because we come from a small-scale, language-based cultural environment, it's something that is generally held across the board – we need to find ways of working with and accommodating differences, working with different culturally-biased people. From my experience one needs to wear all sorts of hats in order to be able to deliver something simultaneously with different cultural groups. I think in the long run it may be very difficult and quite a challenge, but surely one of the ways of doing it is really to make friends with these people. At least for the moment I've been arguing about that, although there are friendships on totally different levels. Like in England, you wouldn't expect to be very close to someone, whereas in Bulgaria, that's the way businesses are run on a daily basis, even more so in the cultural sector – building or exploiting one's friendships is a critical success factor, even for a minor cultural event.

NINA CZEGLEDY:

I would just like to add something in relation to coming from Eastern Europe: we are culturally conditioned to learn other languages, because our languages are not easily accessible. We also have to read world literature because our own literature in our own countries is just now being slowly translated. So we bring these basic things to whatever we do actually, whether it is curatorial or just expanding and collaborating outside.

PAMELA WELLS:

I was just going to say something about audience development. Particularly interesting is that on the Web we don't need to develop audiences. We know there's a whole issue about whether people actually have access to the Internet and how they have access to that and when, and how much it costs. But people are looking at websites all the time, so it's not like galleries trying to get people in the door – people are in the door. But instead of trying to get them into the door, it's like a supermarket, on the cereal aisle, trying to get them to look at your brand. If people are already looking at Websites, it's a matter of how you get them to look at your 'cereal'. It's different because it's a switch as far as marketing and publicity and the business aspect of branding goes.

ILIYANA NEDKOVA:

I think we can possibly still be hopeful that there is a lot of room for filtering through this enormous sea of data that is being produced and refined daily. This is where the curators can step in and be really proactive and 'guides on the side', as I mentioned earlier. People will need these filters and I would trust someone who has done a very intelligent tour around a certain issue that I'm interested in, rather than do it myself.

TAMAS BANOVICH:

I am wondering, who would you envisage as an audience for this kind of community outreach project? Would it be a voyeur, somebody who was going to look at the stream outside this environment? The other thing that I wanted to say, if I was a digital or web artist who is not well connected to a curator, I might see it as a globalised, international conspiracy of friends – impenetrable! [Laughter] So you have to look at it in that sense too. Where is the openness?

ILIYANA NEDKOVA:

There is always this danger of us being accused of being yet another Mafia structure or something similar, but yes, I think we're not really aiming at these extreme forms of partnering here. Back to your first question about who this community-based work is for: I think first and foremost it is for the community that is actually involved in the production. It is really about servicing their needs and that's a big enough audience... sometimes. There is a theory surfacing that we are being broken down into discreet and very small units and we're being targeted by the e-commerce world as well as – as I've tried to indicate here with the www.superchannel.org analysis – by the art world as individuals. So the audience may comprise just one individual at times, and that might be very well justified.

THOMSON & CRAIGHEAD

BERYL GRAHAM:

I would like to introduce Jon Thomson and Alison Craighead. They are media artists who have been making artwork for galleries and for specific sites, and since 1996, have been concentrating on Web-based work. They're currently exhibiting in the 'Art and Money Online' exhibition at Tate Britain. They're also in the exhibition '010101' at the San Francisco Museum of Modern Art. Today they are going to be talking about their artwork and also about some of the production and organisation processes behind it.

JON THOMSON:

Thanks Beryl. What we are going to do is to identify what we think are key works that we've made over the last four years and then we'll talk about an exhibition we did in a gallery last autumn and lastly, about the work we've done for SFMoMA.

ALISON CRAIGHEAD:

I think because you're not our usual audience we thought it might be helpful for you if we just explained how we went about, not making the work, but actually getting what we needed to make the work. So, before we talk about the piece we'll say either if we got sponsorship for it or the partners that we worked with.

JON THOMSON:

It's probably good to say that we work in the gallery and we use the World Wide Web as a place to site our work. I think networked space is something that we're becoming increasingly interested in as artists, but we're going to start by just showing you a work that appeared in the Lux Gallery in 1998, as part of a very short group show called 'The Eyes of March'. It's a work called 'Trigger-Happy' and is a game based on Space Invaders. There is an online version as well, but we're going to show the installation version.

ALISON CRAIGHEAD:

Going back to my original promise, this project was funded by the Arts Council and I think that was a small new media grant.

JON THOMSON:

It was the New Media Projects Fund. [Videogame playing]. The text is 'What is an Author?' by Michel Foucault, and the nine levels of the game take you, in an abridged form, through the whole essay. We chose this essay because we were interested in how present Foucault was in this text that purported the death of authorship.

ALISON CRAIGHEAD:

I think that was something that we were very aware of when we first started working with computers and we were just beginning to think about hypertext and how it was going to change language and authorship. So we decided to work with Foucault because I think he was very eighties and so was 'Space Invaders' for us, and the two somehow fitted together.

JON THOMSON:

When the work is in the gallery, you approach a plinth which contains the projector and there's a game pad on top of the plinth and you just take your place behind it and start playing the game. What we found interesting about this work was the relationship that developed between the active user and the passive viewer, where the active user couldn't really read the text, but was destroying it from the back to the front. Whereas the passive viewer got an overview of the text but was never able to actually read it properly, because the whole thing was just fragmenting in this almost poetic way.

ALISON CRAIGHEAD:

I think that when we've actually taken work that is navigational into a gallery, this is the first time we've felt it was successful. We'd done it before. We started using the terms 'passive viewer' and 'active viewer' and it's very, very important now that when we do anything in a gallery that's navigational, we use this rule of thinking. The audio is taken from number stations. I don't know if you know what number stations are?

JON THOMSON:

They exist in the upper short-wave bands and they are anonymous in so far as governments don't accept that they broadcast at these frequencies. There's a whole series of conspiracy theories that surrounds them because no one will actually admit that they exist. So you tune into them and you hear people just spouting a series of numbers with various musical tones behind and most people believe that they are single-cipher codes being sent. At the moment most of them originate in Central Europe.

ALISON CRAIGHEAD:

And all you need is a good strong radio to find them. They're amazing.

JON THOMSON:

The next piece of work we're going to show is 'Speaking In Tongues'. We were commissioned by Pandemonium, which is the London Festival of Moving Images, in 1998, and for that commission we made a work, which we are going to show you video documentation of. [Video plays]

I suppose from a formal point of view, we were very interested in how our audience might engage with this work. We were interested in it being user-led or navigable, but in a way that wasn't necessarily primarily using a point of contact that was a game pad, a mouse, a joystick or some other button-type device. We found that the rather voyeuristic sense of using the stethoscope to just listen to the wall seemed to work quite well and also people could participate in groups.

ALISON CRAIGHEAD:

There were many things that were interesting about that for us. This was the first time we had set it up but later on we set it up in different venues – Estonia, then later on in Cambridge. What became interesting is, we started off with the recorded data for the first one – just tapes and personal stereos. But then we started using the live network and this is the first time that we really realised we could use live networks within galleries. Another thing that made an impression and we've recognised in our works since then, is that it became very noticeable that there were standard ways that people would use the phone, which is probably very obvious, but since you only ever really listen to your own phone calls, you don't realise quite how universal they are.

JON THOMSON:

So what we would find is that people's conversations would follow a certain pattern where it might be, 'I couldn't get in touch with you because you had your phone switched off. How can I trust you if you haven't got your phone switched on? I don't know where you are.' This would recur a lot. The only obvious absence was a coded reference to things like drug deals. The people who were trying to arrange a deal would know that people could listen to the network and that it is actually a relatively public domain.

So with 'Speaking in Tongues' we felt we were investigating to some extent the way in which the telephone network sounds and how we can listen to it in this proprietary interface that we developed with the stethoscopes. At the same time, we were interested in how it looked as well. We were using the Internet and the World Wide Web, which had emerged in 1994-ish – obviously the Internet was in existence for quite a lot longer. We were beginning to develop web works and with the next piece we're going to show we didn't actually have any funding. We'd managed to buy a computer and get ourselves online. We began to use it a little bit like a studio space where we could try stuff out and we made the next piece of work that we're going to show, called 'Pet Pages', as a result of a surfing overdose where we would come across numerous homepages people had put up about their pets.

ALISON CRAIGHEAD:

At the time this was very important for us because all the discussions that were going on were about the 'virtual' and 'losing yourself'. It was all very sci-fi and it was just a bit of a slam in the head realisation that actually the majority of people were just doing very domestic things online and that a whole culture was evolving very strongly that was about The Homepage. These – we would say you could call them the first 'homesteaders' – were the first people really to really settle down on the Internet.

JON THOMSON:

We would be spending time going to conferences and seminars talking about the impact of global communication technologies and the World Wide Web and how it was going to transform everything about the way we deal with each other and the way we form communities. And around that time, in 1995 and 1996, people didn't use the Internet and they didn't realise that this was the reality of it.

ALISON CRAIGHEAD:

I remember, after all these amazing conferences about all these communities I was going to be involved with and these people I was going to meet, I went out there desperately trying to make friends and I did really, really badly. I would e-mail people and they wouldn't e-mail back. Then I got desperate and I e-mailed a dog called E-wee and actually E-wee is still online: E-wee became my only e-mail correspondent.

JON THOMSON:

[Cicking through the site, which can be found at www.thomson-craighead.net] A lot of these homepages were written in the first person, where the pet would describe the owner. It was often the most effective way of finding out something about the owner's personal story that was colonising these online spaces. These were appearing before e-commerce became a coined phrase and even before Amazon was in full swing.

ALISON CRAIGHEAD:

It taught us a lot, this piece. When we started off, we didn't really have a clue why we were doing it, to be honest. Our main concern was, how could we deal with interface in a more interesting manner? At that point there was no Flash and everything was very square, so we decided to try and mess it up as much as possible by having numerous windows. It is based on the game 'Top Trumps', which is a very English thing, I think, because when we talk about it in other places, people don't always get it. Does everyone here know what 'Top Trumps' is? It was a seventies or eighties thing and it's been coming back recently. You would get cards of say, Super Heroes, tanks, racing cars, and then you would split the set and play them against other people.

JON THOMSON:

We felt that a deck of cards was a fairly obvious metaphor to use for the interface without it having to be within one window. So you would know how to use it intuitively and it would be using the operating system the way in which the operating system represents information more than just designing within the browser, and that interested us. Just to move quickly to Pepper's homepage: this was pretty much the first time we'd come across a MIDI-file.
[Website plays with sound]

ALISON CRAIGHEAD:

We later went on to find out – and I'm sure you will all know this – that MIDI-files colonise the Web. They are everywhere! At first we couldn't believe that people would actually decide to choose to soundtrack themselves – their representation – with a MIDI-file.

JON THOMSON:

What people would tend to do is visit huge repositories of these MIDI-files, which are very, very data light conversions of music which can be downloaded very quickly. People would also be spending time travelling to various websites so that they could grab animated gifs to decorate their homepage. So this became a little bit like 'Ikea' I guess, but online.

ALISON CRAIGHEAD:

I still have trouble categorising an animated gif. But in trying to make a reference, it was somewhere between a tattoo and a fridge magnet – a very strange phenomenon in how we wished to decorate ourselves online.

JON THOMSON:

So we immediately began to look at transcripts of chat rooms in conjunction with animated gifs and MIDI-files, which led us to make this piece of work called 'Weightless', which was made with support from Artec. This is a purely online work and doesn't exist in the gallery. [Website plays]

ALISON CRAIGHEAD:

I think, at this stage, I was really watching too much daytime television and hanging around in chat rooms too much as well. We started to think about what could be tele-visual online, because there were talks at the beginning about television and streaming media. We started to think about what would be the equivalent of say, the test card or the opening tune – so this is it. If you go in using Explorer, you get a big 'E' and if you go in using Netscape, you get a big 'N'.

JON THOMSON:

We wanted to make an environment in which the interface existed in one page. We were interested in hypertext functioning in a way that was coherent rather than just linear and always branching off. So you would click onto something and go to another page and click somewhere else and just always be making choices. So although this is actually the same kind of thing, it never leaves this page.

So in this instance we were trying to contrive a notionally televisual format where the transcripts from the chat rooms become like sub-titles, the animated gifs give the image and the MIDI-files, the soundtracks. Also, what was very important to us at this time was that we were beginning to manipulate existing resources rather than continuing to fill up this burgeoning database that is the World Wide Web with our own representations. It seemed that actually more than ever, and this obviously has a lot of precedence in art history, the Internet provides an environment where appropriation then manipulation, became a lot more like traditional notions of representation, because it was such an endless and endlessly-mutable database that we were drawing from.

ALISON CRAIGHEAD:

I think that is probably one of the most important things in our work. I mean, at this stage it was fascinating, for me at least, just to watch the breakdown or the development of language through the Internet. You can see that already people are shortening words and now, if you look at it, it has sped up incredibly with text messaging, SMS and pagers. But at this stage it was like looking at hieroglyphics and it was happening so quickly. Already people were beginning to punctuate their language with these cutesy images, which is now traditional and goes on and on and on. This was 1998 and I think you can see already that it looks old-fashioned in the way that people are communicating here. [Website plays] We have to say that this piece does make us feel vaguely ill. When we were making it we spent months working on an interface that would be fluid and ever-changing, and the build up of this cutesyness and music would really make us feel physically ill by the end of the day.

[...]

JON THOMSON:

We're going to show you two more pieces of work that are more recent. The first is documentation of an exhibition we did last autumn called 'Telephony'. We were still interested in this big network that is the telecommunications network. You could probably characterise a lot of the work we've made over the last four years as being about looking at the way in which we all relate to and use networks and new communications tools, and what impact they have on our lives. The work 'Telephony' was a gallery work. It was made with support from corporate sponsorship that we actually secured from Siemens.

ALISON CRAIGHEAD:

Siemens, Orange – and also Becks. We really needed it in order to do this piece because it would be phenomenally expensive otherwise, as you will see in a minute.

JON THOMSON:

It's a very simple audio work. The documentation you're going to look at is actually charting two pieces of work, which will just unravel once the documentation is played through, which again is only about three-and-a-half minutes.

ALISON CRAIGHEAD:

It was placed in a small commercial gallery in London called Mobile Home. [Video plays]

JON THOMSON:

So we put both works together because we felt that in an audio sense they complemented one another. The two distinctions that we'd make are firstly that you had the grid of mobile phones that would be lying dormant in the gallery if no one was there, while this supermarket music played that was based on the Nokia tune.

ALISON CRAIGHEAD:

And the supermarket music was really based in the hallway and stairs. There's a long stairway up, so you would just hear this playing in the background as you walked in and climbed the stairs up to the gallery.

JON THOMSON:

So you would pop into the gallery space and there would be phones available (or you could just use your own) and a list of numbers. You could dial the grid of phones which would then call forwards to each other and begin to gather weight and play fragments, again based on the Nokia tune. The more people that dialed in, the more layered it became. If there was just a single visitor to the gallery, it would be a single dialogue with the user dialing the grid of phones and listening to the harmonic relationship with the supermarket music. However, we also had the Universal Master Clock playing through a lie-detector on the other side of the gallery. This is the second work, in which the commercially available truth-verification software called 'Truster' is live-testing this clock that comes through the Internet. The Universal Master Clock tells the truth, as opposed to the reports on the wall, which are from other speaking clocks that weren't telling the truth according to the software. So, for example, the British Speaking Clock was prone to exaggeration.

ALISON CRAIGHEAD:

And the Irish one was very confused.

JON THOMSON:

And the New York Weather and Time Check was very unsure of much of what it said. Ironically, the Universal Master Clock always delivers itself via real audio with a time lag of at least six seconds. We were simply trying to undermine these two technologies by putting them together.

ALISON CRAIGHEAD:

This lie-detector software is used a lot in the Arab States, in court cases or corporate cases, and its actual end result can end up with you getting sacked or getting your hand chopped off. It is believed in and trusted – like its name, 'Truster'.

JON THOMSON:

It's the cheaper alternative to the Polygraph, which is the more traditional lie-detector which tests sweat and heart rate.

ALISON CRAIGHEAD:

And I think it's only three per cent less accurate than the Polygraph. Just one more thing: when you start working with mobile phones or anything that's new, in a lot of ways you're learning as you go along. What happened with the telephone piece that was really lovely and exciting for us was the fact that – especially at the opening – people who had their own mobile phones were dialing into the piece. Then, throughout the rest of the run of the show, people would just go into the gallery and press 'redial' and then our piece would end up calling back people who had visited it. We didn't realise this was going to happen at all, and it was actually something that was very interesting. So people were telling us, 'your piece called us again!'

JON THOMSON:

Again, it was very important to us that we were using a live network, where our work is perhaps presented in the gallery in close proximity to its audience, but the work itself has a distance. You can be far away from it or near it and it just exists and hangs in this existing network, which is topographical and real.

ALISON CRAIGHEAD:

Yes, and it was really nice that it could actually come in and maybe there would be somebody crouching and shouting into the phone and they would be calling their friend – because there was a free network connection there. Yet still the piece could exist around them within that constraint and that made us both feel quite happy.

JON THOMSON:

The last piece is called 'E-Poltergeist' and it was commissioned by SFMoMA for the online part of the exhibition '010101: Art In Technological Times'. We spent a long while considering what we should do for this in terms of creating a Net-specific work – a work that exists purely online for access through a browser. We had become very, very interested – on the back of our surfing experiences through Geocities – in a whole host of sites. One particular site we accessed was a suicide note, which surprised us because it was a suicide note that had advertised itself through HTML to search engines using meta-tags. It struck us as a very complex attempt at communication.

ALISON CRAIGHEAD:

And so we were really shocked and struck by this and we spent a lot of time looking at it and we started to think, 'is this a one-off or is this happening often?' So what we ended up doing was going to a search engine and putting in different questions or criteria to try and find more and an actual conversation seemed to develop.

JON THOMSON:

Well, rather a monologue. We were keying things in like, 'I want to kill myself,' or 'please help me,' 'help me, I want to end it all.' We found that it created a monologue and that the consistent results that we got from these narrative fragments almost wrote themselves; they had a certain tenor. So it led us to make 'E-Poltergeist', which is quite hard to present. It's easier to use – it is an intervention in the browser, it's very durational. It basically loads up a time-line. It loads up no interface particularly. You're simply taken to the Yahoo search engine, and over a short period of time, the browser starts to misbehave itself a little and you get these narrative fragments coming in through search engine results. What was most important for us in making this work, was this way in which we could use live data – live search engine data – to construe a single monologue.

ALISON CRAIGHEAD:

Another formal thing we were very interested in was the fact that the portal was becoming a bigger and bigger burden in the sense that once you make a piece of work, then you have to design an interface. So we were very interested in trying to have no visible interface.

JON THOMSON:

Although the work exists on the SFMoMA site, it was designed to be encountered as an intervention. If you visit our site, we encourage people to take the Yahoo logo and to create links to this work surreptitiously from their own websites. We were conscious that it would have a different impact if it was encountered inadvertently.

ALISON CRAIGHEAD:

We now have maybe two or three pieces of work that we have instructions on our website on how to host as an intervention, because that's really how we prefer these works to come across ('CNN Interactive' is the other one). It's very difficult to explain this because it's very much about using it and feeling that there is another presence. It's quite a cheesy metaphor to have a ghost in a machine, very well trodden.

JON THOMSON:

But it's also real. It's live data. It's on a search engine so it changes.

ALISON CRAIGHEAD:

We just ask the questions and it changes all the time. So this piece changes as the Yahoo results change and the input is purely what comes out of asking the questions. So, 'I want to kill myself, my Pentium has crashed,' will lie next to something more desperate, a desperate plea, but it's just a search engine. It's just a machine that asks the questions then we, as the users, give the answers. The other thing that is interesting for us about this work is the fact that there are different layers. So you could either come and just get the flashing, blinking feeling that there is a poltergeist or a ghost in the machine, or if you actually go further and explore and click through the search engine results, it can actually take you to some very different and interesting parts of the web.

JON THOMSON:

So it is at once a delivery of a piece of durational narrative, and also an arcane search engine. It is quite hard to leave the work as well, especially if you're using a PC and Explorer: usually you have to restart the machine. We were also interested in creating this closed-circuit loop because it felt important to us that the way in which the computer functions and the fallibility of computers could possibly be brought into the same fold as our original metaphor. So as the machine malfunctions, it becomes part of the actual work itself and the content.

ALISON CRAIGHEAD:

And also the whole architecture of just using the computer: and we were shocked at how upset people got at the idea of having to restart.

JON THOMSON:

No one actually told us that Yahoo and Intel were partners in the SFMoMA exhibition and Intel had issues with our work, which was a shame because we ended up having to compromise a little bit on the '010101' site. But because we wanted to try and reach an audience, we felt we couldn't pull the piece. Also, it was a very important opportunity for us.

ALISON CRAIGHEAD:

I think that's very interesting as well, because when you start having to work with new technology, then obviously it is very expensive and to put on a big show like '010101' takes a lot of money. So you end up – this is our first experience of it actually – with a situation where there wasn't a sponsor, it was a 'partner' and it was quite shocking that when the press release went out, we had no idea that we were being promoted by the words, 'Intel Presents...'. We weren't actually told of this, which also is something that I think is going to occur more and more and will become a bit of an issue.

MARK TRIBE:

I hadn't heard about this. Can you tell us how your work was compromised?

ALISON CRAIGHEAD:

Well, we had a pretty horrible week actually. It was maybe two weeks before the show was to open and then we got a message saying that the partner had issues. At that stage we didn't know what or who the partner was and it was a very, very uncomfortable situation.

JON THOMSON:

They didn't like the fact that you couldn't leave the work very easily and that it would dispose of the '010101' interface as it began to progress. We'd actually flagged this up over the course of the year saying, 'Are you sure you want to take this work?'

ALISON CRAIGHEAD:

Because we offered a selection of works and we were very impressed that they took something that we felt was quite difficult.

JON THOMSON:

We were hugely excited.

ALISON CRAIGHEAD:

We felt it was quite difficult to place within a portal and we did bring this up and deliver the finished piece quite a few months before.

MARK TRIBE:

So it crashes the browser?

JON THOMSON:

Yes, and if you're using PC and Explorer then you have to 'End Task' to leave the browser or you have to restart the machine. What we ended up having to do was to make the work stoppable and to warn people through a series of alerts that some terrible thing was about to happen and that you would have to quit your browser.

ALISON CRAIGHEAD:

So we had to put warnings on. Of course, the whole idea of having a poltergeist where you can go, 'Okay, here's the Go-Away-Poltergeist button' – it's obviously compromising. So we dealt with it in terms of saying, 'this is a demo of the piece' and we used the language of software to try and deal with it. But I have to say it was a very horrible situation.

MARK TRIBE:

Did you get the sense that the curator, who I guess is Benjamin Weil, initially liked the work the way it was, and then got caught between the interests of the sponsor?

JON THOMSON:

Absolutely.

ALISON CRAIGHEAD:

He was trying his absolute best, but it was just really horrible. Then we found out that the other partner who we hadn't been told about, was Yahoo. They weren't happy with us either and we had to change the name of the piece.

MARK TRIBE:

What was the previous name?

ALISON CRAIGHEAD:

'Do you Yahoo?'

MARK TRIBE:

So they compromised your artistic integrity to keep the corporate money?

JON THOMSON:

To some extent, yes.

ALISON CRAIGHEAD:

Well, the thing that actually was most upsetting to be honest, was not the fact that this was happening (which was upsetting), but the fact that we had something like two weeks before the show opened, whereas we had delivered, maybe three months before. So that was actually the part which I felt was bad.

[...]

JON THOMSON:

We don't consider ourselves to be hackers or whatever terms are used. We sometimes make things that play around with the browser a little bit. In the work that we have at Tate Britain at the moment we add to the CNN news site, but it's hardly an outrageous attack on their website. We are interested in very specific things. We're interested in just this idea of 'soundtracking' news and how it impacts on the way in which we receive what is inevitably biased reportage; news is always biased in some respects, wherever it comes from. We were interested in the fiction-fact-infotainment blur, yet people immediately always latch onto the fact that we added to an existing site and perhaps it's a little bit naughty. But it's not that bad.

ALISON CRAIGHEAD:

Yes, and what are CNN going to do to us?

JON THOMSON:

'E-Poltergeist' is the same. So you have to quit your browser – it's not the end of the world!

ALISON CRAIGHEAD:

Let's just think about it. We made a piece where you had to quit the browser and if you were on a Pentium then you would have to restart. Now, let's think about say, what Hans Haacke does; let's think about the Venice Biennale.

JON THOMSON:

He drills up floors.

ALISON CRAIGHEAD:

Yes, I mean, this is highly extreme. But someone has to restart their computer? I started to realise that actually galleries are more precious about their Web presence than they are about their gallery space. They are happier to take risks within the galleries than they are on the Web, when you get down to big institutions. That's amazing!

VUK COSIC:

Why did you work with SFMoMA? You could have just published this site yourself.

ALISON CRAIGHEAD:

Yes. The thing is, I really like galleries. We're traditionally trained. I went to art school and studied drawing and painting. I love going to galleries. I like the institutions and I like showing in them. Obviously, you normally think you can foresee the problems beforehand. There are some pieces that we just do on our website because that's an interesting area to work in. So for us, we're very happy to be shown in galleries.

JON THOMSON:

We want to reach audiences and the audiences are different if they're institutional, than if they are people who just come across your website online, and we just want to be in dialogue and to try to be part of a group of people who are thinking about these issues, and the institutions that we've worked with form part of that strategy for us.

CLAIRE DOHERTY:

I suppose the most obvious thing that comes out of it is the nature of the branding in relation to the institutions that you're working with, the partners they're working with, and then of yourselves as individuals and artists. I suppose it's actually where you begin to align those things and where the core of branding in the end is value systems. At the core of that are the values that they stand by. I wonder when you, as individual artists, have your values, whether they can be aligned and when you have to give in to something to meet the needs of a greater brand? Are there points when you say, 'well actually, that value doesn't stand'?

JON THOMSON:

It varies. I think it has to be taken on a case-by-case basis.

ALISON CRAIGHEAD:

Yes. I mean, with SFMoMA, we outlined exactly what we were going to do in a proposal. It got accepted and then we delivered. We didn't pull any punches. We weren't naughty artists. We didn't change the piece at the last minute and for me, with them agreeing and having discussions about it, I was packing my bag ready to go off to San Francisco and then the phone call came. So, for me I didn't see it as an issue. I'd worked with Benjamin before and I really respect his curatorial take, so this was like a bolt out of the blue for us – which is maybe a little bit naïve, but then I think you have to get experience somehow!

MATTHEW GANSALLO:

I'm not obsessed with trying to define art, as it were, but I wanted to know – as you've shown us a range of work from what you have in the galleries on the wall to a specific type of online work – whether you can define your practice, or is it indefinable?

ALISON CRAIGHEAD:

Our practice is definable. We see ourselves as artists who use readymades, who manipulate existing data.

JON THOMSON:

We are very interested in the impact that new communication tools are having on the way in which we all perceive and engage with the world around us and we use the context that the art world provides as a way in which we can engage in this way. We don't make films in a broad, mainstream, cinematic sense. We're not scientists. We're not an e-commercial venture or a commercial venture. It's what we're not that defines the space that is art in many ways, I think.

PETER RIDE:

I was wondering about the way in which you define yourself in a relation to the practice of external curators, because I think you've represented yourselves as very autonomous artists who have a clear sense of where you're going with your work. The jury is still out on whether curators are relevant, in terms of what lots of people in this sector do. Sometimes it is executive production – you've given examples of that with the fundraising – sometimes it is as a catalyst to generate ideas and sometimes it's risk-management. With SFMoMA you've bought up a really interesting example of the way in which you have to work with a curator and the edifice of an institution. As it seems to me that you're very clear about where your projects are going, what do you like to get out of a relationship with a curator or a curatorial team, and do you set the parameters of that relationship, or do they set the parameters and you work within them?

ALISON CRAIGHEAD:

Every relationship is different. I think discussion is always really important. Everything we do is slightly different, so just as long as we end up making something. A lot of the time what happens is, we make something, we put it on the Website and maybe someone will come along and say, 'I find that interesting. I'd like to represent it in some way.' Then we start talking. So maybe some people ask for an adaptation of a Web piece into a gallery.

JON THOMSON:

Basically we're a peer group and we do different things in a very similar field and that, to us, is the strength of being able to work with curators – to be able to develop ideas for exhibitions. Sometimes a curator will have a very particular idea of what they want to present in terms of an exhibition and we need to fit into that. Sometimes it might be the exact converse. It varies tremendously.

ALISON CRAIGHEAD:

And sometimes you'll have discussions about a show and maybe it will end up being about the particular take that the curator has. I'm thinking particularly about e-commerce, because Julian Stallabrass actually came around and started talking to us about e-commerce and art and money. Actually, I have to say that 'E-Poltergeist' came from that initial conversation, even though it went on somewhere else, but it made us realise about how the home or the intensely private side of the Internet is so connected with the commercial side.

JON THOMSON:

One thing that's very important to us is the notion that people can identify similarities within the diversity of the practices that exist within this term 'new media' – although it isn't new media – rather than difference. Because things are often defined in terms of their differences I think, and not always to a productive end.

KATHY RAE HUFFMAN:

What I wanted to say is that you made a contract with SFMoMA. You presented a proposal and they accepted it. This is a very formal process. It's a very important institution garnering mega-support from the high-tech industry which it needs to sustain the museum. This was all agreed upon contractually and, like Mark Tribe, I'm just a bit distressed that you changed the work. What did they offer you? Did you change the contract or did you just back down?

JON THOMSON:

We backed down.

ALISON CRAIGHEAD:

We sat and talked about what we were going to do. We talked to friends, curators or anyone that was about – and we just made the decision that we were going to back down because otherwise we were going to be pulled from the show.

KATHY RAE HUFFMAN:

But that's censorship! It was censorship and they are liable for damages in this case. But there's an issue at hand here and it's a very important issue – artists shouldn't be controlled by sponsors.

BERYL GRAHAM:

I'm sorry to interrupt because this is a very interesting conversation. This isn't censorship, but it is lunch I'm afraid, and we do have to break here. Thank you very much to Jon and Alison.

[Audience applause]

MARK TRIBE

SARAH COOK:

Mark is the co-founder of Rhizome, which is a net-art and digital art resource based in New York City. Rhizome has a vibrant mailing list that many of you probably subscribe to.

MARK TRIBE:

I want to talk briefly about how I became interested in net-art and what drew me to it in the first place, and then discuss three projects that I'm involved in that connect with different issues of curatorial practice in the sphere of new media.

I first got interested in the Net as a space for art making when I was a grad student getting my MFA in Visual Art at the University of California, San Diego. Like a lot of people, my practice evolved from really traditional media like painting, print-making and photography, to playing around with video and installation, and then I got into doing happenings and social events. In 1992 and 1993, I started to become curious about cyberspace and the Internet, which I had just started hearing about at that time. One of the things that I did was I went out and bought all the cyber-punk novels that I could find and started reading. It seemed like there was a common denominator – a common thread – among a lot of these novels, like William Gibson's 'Neuromancer', 'Snow-Crash' by Neil Stephenson and 'When Gravity Fails' by Mark Effinger; the list is actually pretty long. That was this notion of a virtual reality as a networked consensual hallu-cination – a real space that you can inhabit and where more and more significant experiences and transactions would take place. And as someone who was doing art in social spaces – parking lots and beaches and airports – it just seemed to me that this was a really interesting place to make art. Then in 1994, when I stumbled across 'Mosaic' – somebody was talking about it on the BBS or on User-Net – it was Eureka! Suddenly there was an inter-active, multimedia tool that we could use that combined, not only hypertext, but also images, moving images and sound. Suddenly it moved beyond text.

I think what really attracted me to working online more than anything else was the idea of direct access to audiences. As a graduate student I was pretty intimidated by the notion of having to make my way in the art world. I wondered if I would have to move to New York and start going to galleries and openings in order to try and convince a gallerist to show my work. I thought, well, with the Internet I can just put it up there and people can see it without me having to go through all those gatekeepers.

So that was a long time ago. Now, seven years later, net-art has gone through a period of being really isolated from the mainstream art world. It evolved as a parallel art world with its own discourse networks, exhibition venues, events and publications. But suddenly, in the last year or so, it started to be rapidly assimilated into the mainstream art world. Funders are now devoting resources to net-art, and museums and galleries are exhibiting it. In the face of this I think we have to deal with a lot of pretty serious contradictions, because the impulses that attracted me and most other people to the Net earlier on, run directly counter to this assimilation process. These powerfully-entrenched institutions have a lot of power and they wield it in problematic ways.

I find myself starting to engage now in different kinds of curatorial practice and asking myself, 'What does it mean, as an artist, to curate?' I'm feeling ambivalent about that, certainly not wanting to be pigeonholed. A lot of other artists have crossed back and forth across that line: Peter Weibel and Jeffrey Shaw at ZKM; Gerfried Stocker at Ars Electronica; Jon Ippolito at the Guggenheim. I wonder what happens to one as an artist after one starts curating? I guess I will find out.

The three projects that I want to talk about are 'Rhizome.org', 'Net-Ephemera' – which is a show that I just curated in a small gallery in New York – and 'Agenda for a Landscape', which is a show that will be coming up at the New Museum (in New York) next year.

[Slide] What we're looking at now while I talk is an interface to Rhizome's archives and content called 'Every Image'. It's a screensaver and we're looking at a web-based demo of it, but you can download it off our website. It was made by Alex Galloway, our director of content and technology – he's the editor of Rhizome and the guy who does all the programming and development.

Rhizome started out as an e-mail list in February 1996. I was living in Berlin and started it because at the time there wasn't really any place to have a focused discussion about new media art in general or net-art in particular. There was Nettime, which was sort of the model for Rhizome, which is more broadly focused on critical discourse and theory of network practice, but not really focused in on artistic practice. I felt that there was a need for a space that in being focused, could be comprehensive. My goal was really to connect a lot of the different local communities. I was living in Berlin and going to festivals such as the Dutch Electronic Art Festival in Rotterdam and ISEA and Ars Electronica in Linz, and realising that that was the only way that people from these different local communities could find out what was going on. So someone like Machiko Kusahara would come all the way from Tokyo just to find out what people were doing in Kyoto for example, or people would congregate face-to-face and one of the common denominators in all these different kinds of communities was that we all had e-mail and access to the Web. So I thought, well, let's use it to foster a conversation. Not only to exchange information, but more importantly, to construct and develop a critical dialogue. I didn't feel that these conferences provided a sustained enough conversational environment in which to really develop a vocabulary to think about the aesthetics, the theoretical ramifications, and the political issues that intersect with doing work online.

Shortly after starting Rhizome, I moved to New York, basically because I had more access to resources there. We separated the initial list, which is just an unmoderated free-for-all, into two tiers, two levels. That's 'Rhizome Raw' and 'Rhizome Digest'. 'Rhizome Raw' is totally unfiltered and with very, very high traffic at this point – anywhere from ten to fifty posts a day, depending on the day and the intensity of the conversation. 'Rhizome Digest' is once a week and what we do is filter out the conversation on Raw, take what we think are the most relevant posts, and combine them into one message and then send that out to people who prefer that mode. The Digest mode grew very quickly, whereas Raw grew very, very slowly. Raw has about five hundred subscribers and Digest has about five thousand.

In the summer of 1996, we started archiving selected posts from Raw in a database that was accessible online. That was the beginning of what we now call 'The Rhizome

Text-Base'. One of the things that we started to do very early was to index all of what we call the text objects in a very consistent way, with keywords identifying what type of text it is – whether it's a review, an interview, an announcement or a commentary – and associating URLs, dates, names, places and images. We make a thumbnail image that illustrates the text and links to a site that is somehow relevant and provides context.

As a gateway to our site we have at this point about thirty different little works of net-art submitted by artists in the community [known as Splashpages]. There's really no formal structure to this; we don't really solicit them. People just send them to us from time to time and if we like them, we put them up. If we don't, then we say, 'Thanks, but no thanks.' [Slide] I'll just show this as an example of a totally non-curated or unformulated exhibition environment. Actually, we're getting more and more submissions now, so we'll have to figure out a way to formalise it and maybe set up some selection criteria.

Then a couple of years later, in 1999, we started archiving works of net-art themselves. We call this the 'Art-Base'. The impulse to start archiving net-art came when we started to realise that a lot of the projects that had been discussed on Rhizome in 1996 and 1997 had vanished. One example was Akke Wagenaar's 'Hiroshima Project' that she did when she was at the Kunsthochschule für Medien in Köln – the work was just gone. I think she had left the KHM and got a job somewhere else, stopped making net-art and the new systems administrator just deleted it – and there goes art history!

So, realising that it's really problematic for a lot of reasons to archive net-art, we nonetheless thought it was important for somebody to start saving this stuff. Then we realised as we started doing this, that a lot of artists didn't want us to save copies of their work. In a certain sense, in cloning it and putting a copy on our servers, we were killing it because the work is perhaps! interactive by nature and it evolves over time, or simply that the artists don't want their work to be frozen. Although in the 'Art-Base' we do allow people to update their projects, nonetheless, a lot of pieces change every day. So we decided to have two different types of works archived in the 'Art-Base' – linked objects and cloned objects. Linked objects are much as they sound – projects where we just store metadata – information about the work, the title, the URL, the artist's name, the day it was created, the date that it was archived, key words, categorical information, what technology it uses, a statement by the artist, and the artist's bio.

The cloned objects contain all that and also a copy of the work itself, which can be updated. Usually what we like to do is show the old version and then a later version, then a later version and so on. We're just starting to get update requests and to figure out how to deal with that. Another issue that comes up with cloning is obsolescence. As we know, the technology that most of these works use is changing so fast. So we really had to wrangle with that and through a lot of conversations – especially with Jon Ippolito at the Guggenheim, who is working on a variable media initiative – we've come up with a schemed set of tactics and strategies for approaching issues of obsolescence. [Slide] There's a whole bunch of content in the 'Art-Base' about obsolescence, but you have to actually submit an object to get to it.

There are four preservation strategies. One is documentation, which is simply making screen charts, or maybe creating a quick-time movie and click-through of the project, and adding interviews with the artists and ephemera related to the production of the work. It is not that satisfying a solution, but we found that in archiving, everything involves compromises really.

The second strategy would be migration. So let's say something was written in HTML 2.0 – a lot of those tags no longer work in Netscape 6. They are depreciated, obsolete. So what you can do is run a Perl script that replaces all the depreciated tags with the new ones. Of course, that only works for certain kinds of projects.

The next, more radical step would be emulation. So, as much as you can emulate an Intel operating system or a Windows operating system in a Macintosh environment by using say, Virtual PC, or emulate Atari games on a PC, in 2020 we'll be able to emulate Windows 2000 on whatever the current operating system is. Then you could install IE5 and Flash 5 – or whatever the appropriate plug-ins are – and theoretically run the work. But even so, that may not work for a lot of projects. Take for example Mark Napier's 'Shredder', which shreds other websites. Well, in a world in which HTML is perhaps completely obsolete, the shredder wouldn't work. So maybe the concept of letting people submit network addresses and mix up and shred the results, could be reinterpreted and applied in a totally new technological environment. The problem is, how do you do this if you don't know what's most important about the work – and if you don't have explicit permission from the artists?

So what we do in the case of cloned objects, is ask artists to fill out a really lengthy multi-page questionnaire on our website in which we explain all these possible preservation strategies and then ask them to say what is most important about the work. Is it the hues of the colours? Is it the way in which the interactivity functions? Is it simply the concept? Is it the fact that you're using readymade technology or customised technology? We try to get at the grain of the work so that when it comes time to actually do something about obsolescence, we feel we have the information and permission that's necessary. A lot of the artists will say, 'No, you can't document it, you can't migrate it, you can't emulate it and you can't reinterpret it.' In which case the work would then exist simply as the metadata: as the title and original URL and description, bio and thumbnail – that's it.

Of course 'Art-Base' is a totally grass-roots archive. We don't go out and invite people. Sometimes we do send out casual invitations, but it's really a DIY thing. Artists come to the site and say, 'I want to submit this project.' So it's very much of an opt-in environment. The concept is to be inclusive, rather than exclusive – to be the opposite of a curated museum collection which is defined more by what is excluded than by what's perhaps included – and to be as comprehensive as possible. So, in an ideal world we would have eventually so much work that you could really get a sense of what was going on in net-art at a given time.

The technology that we use is one hundred per cent open-source. The operating system is Linux, the web-server is Apache, and the database is MySOL. The middle ware is PHP. The scripting is Perl and HTML. There is no Flash, no Cold Fusion, no Oracle, no Windows and no Microsoft, which is largely because it works better and it's free. But also because we're more philosophically aligned with open-source.

One cool thing about the 'Art-Base' is that it uses the same database platform and metadata structures as the 'Text-Base', so when you do searches – say you do a query on cyberfeminism or something like that – then it will come up with a mix of art projects and texts that connect with it in some way or other. Or you can do a search on an artist (for example, Shu Lea Cheang) and find things that were written about her, or by her and artworks by her. So it is an attempt to embed the work within the context of the critical discourse that surrounds it at the time.

We do have a strong advisory panel with people who are involved in new media around the world, to guide us in making decisions. We've tried to establish collaborations and associations with other people that are involved in similar initiatives, like the archive at the Daniel Langlois

Foundation in Montreal. The CIAO Initiative (Conceptual and Intermedia Arts Online) is a set of different libraries and archives that are dealing with archiving this stuff, with Jon Ippolito at the Guggenheim. They are just starting to figure out a way to link V2's archive from all their activities in Rotterdam, with ours. So, for example, if you found a reference to Steve Dietz on the V2 website, you could then link to or pull in content from the Rhizome 'Art-Base' or 'Text-Base'.

I guess my main thought about Rhizome in connection with curatorial practice is this notion of filtering rather than curating, of having multiple layers ranging from totally open to progressively filtered in different ways. I think filtration is fairly necessary in order to help people find what they're looking for, and to create a coherent content resource. But at the same time, what we do really reverses the traditional paradigm of curating, or publishing, in which you have a few people creating content from many instances. We're trying to create a many-to-many communication environment.

On to 'Net Ephemera'. Last fall I was approached by Michelle Thursz, who is the director of a really small, marginal, fairly temporary gallery space in New York called Moving Image Gallery (MIG), which, I think, is unfortunately about to close. She asked me if I would like to do a show. There are a bunch of galleries in New York that are showing new media right now. I think by far the strongest programme is at Postmasters and they show the most interesting and ambitious work. But also Sandra Gering is showing work by John Simon and Jordan Crandall and a few others. Universal Concept Unlimited is showing Joseph Nechvatal and a few other artists and even some mainstream, more or less blue-chip galleries are starting to show new media. So there are a lot of spaces now opening up in the commercial gallery world for new media artists in New York. But MIG is actually one of the only ones that is devoted exclusively to new media and it was also interesting to me just because of the limitations, because there's a lack of resources there – there was no money for the show and it's a very small space.

Initially I was looking at the different ways in which curators had been trying to solve the problem of how to put art that was made to be experienced online in the physical space of the gallery. You have a lot of botched attempts – like the 2000 Whitney Biennial in which they just projected works on the wall without really discussing it with the artists much – to more sensitive approaches, like what Steve Deitz is doing at the Walker. The approach that I favoured, ideally, was what we would call the 'Data Dynamics' approach – where you invite the artist to make a work that bridges the physical and the virtual, rather than taking work that was meant to be experienced offline and just sticking it into the physical space. I didn't have the resources to do that, and also I really wanted to do a large group show. There are a lot of really great net-artists working in New York right now – probably forty or fifty – for whom the Net is their primary medium. I wanted to do a large, almost comprehensive, group show. I was also very interested in the process of making the work. I thought that was something that was largely invisible in most of the exhibitions I'd seen, and I have an ongoing interest in documentation. So I decided to show – as the title of the show implies – ephemera, relating to the making of the work. Things like drawings, diagrams, notes, flyers, postcards, receipts, cheques and things like that, that would shed light on the process of making the work, and what the artist was thinking, what the significance of the work is in the artist's mind. [Slide] The show includes work by twenty-five artists. I asked each artist to provide one thing on paper, and it had to be eight-and-a-half by eleven inches or smaller – that's our version of A4. I then stuck them in a line on the wall.

[...]

Another train of thought that intersected with my decision-making process sprang from being asked repeatedly how or whether net-art was being sold and how it would eventually be sold in galleries. Because today there really is no commercial market for net-art. Net-art was born out of a utopian moment in a gift economy. It wasn't about selling the work. It was very much in the spirit of conceptual art, Fluxus and other kinds of relatively radical artistic practice – it was resisting the commodification and objectification of the artwork. At the same time, artists want to pay the rent and doing day jobs like web design and database development is maybe not preferable to being able to live off just making your work, in the way that a few artists already are, such as John Simons. So one of my stock answers was, 'Well, it will probably be commodified much in the way that conceptual art, earthworks and performance art have been – which is through the ephemera.' So that was in the back of my mind.

[...]

So I'll move on to talk briefly about a project that's coming up. I don't have any visuals for it. It is called 'Agenda for a Landscape'. The New Museum has opened up a media lounge in their basement. It used to be their public access gallery – the part of the museum that you could get into for free just by walking in off the street. Now it is dedicated to doing new media projects and in this case I was invited to do a show as a guest curator. I am taking the 'Data Dynamics' approach to the problem by inviting Leah Gillam to do a project that is experience-able online and offline at the same time. Just to quickly describe the project: she's interested in the narrative of the Mars Pathfinder Expedition. NASA sent a space probe up to Mars a few years ago and it landed on the surface and sent down a small, microwave oven-sized robot that crawled around the surface, took pictures and sent them back. The name of this robot was 'Sojourner', named after Sojourner Truth, who was an abolitionist in the period before slavery was abolished in the States. Leah was interested in the notion of the master/slave narrative playing through this space mission. So that's the allegorical fulcrum of the work and the plan is, if we can pull together the funding, to create a tele-robot of sorts that will navigate around a media landscape that she constructs in the gallery and that you will be able to navigate online. Sort of in the vein of Ken Goldberg's 'Telegarden'. In this case, I see my role as curator, not so much as someone who is pulling together a lot of different work or acting as an artist, but more as a producer – a facilitator – somebody who is helping the artist realise her idea by putting her in touch with funders, robot engineers and different artists and people that have worked in the media. I am helping her to explore this new technology as a way of working.

[Audience applause]

SARAH COOK:

I'm curious about the terms used in your 'Art-Base' – your archival search terms. For us at BALTIC in terms of developing a new programme, we're just now considering how we're going to archive our activities. We're not going to be an institution that collects art, and so we have many ideas about the value of a 'paperless' or virtual archive versus that of a real archive. I know you said that you've got a lot of people who you're working with as advisors. My question is about the search terms you use and how you did the indexing.

MARK TRIBE:

When we first started archiving text objects we had to come up with a list of key words that we would use to list different types. That became our metadata structure and then we transposed it from text objects onto art objects. The problem we then identified was that it was fairly idiosyncratic and didn't conform to the various metadata standards that are out there. We realised that there is this huge field of librarians and archivists who are very, very obsessed with consistency and compatibility – the idea being that if all of the different libraries and archives out there share the same metadata standards, then you can do searches across them and somebody who learns to use one then knows how to use them all. So now we're starting to wrangle with the problem of how to match the way that we index to the way that other people index. We're finding, in fact, that the problem with adhering to standards is that the standards weren't created to deal with this kind of work. In fact, our system works a lot better for this kind of work because it was tailor-made. So maybe what will end up happening is we'll go to XML or something like that and then set some interpretative layer that allows our structure to be mapped onto or connected with other structures.

SARAH COOK:

I'm supposed to ask you about your T-shirt?

MARK TRIBE:

This t-shirt was given to me by James Buckhouse from San Francisco. He's the guy that curated the screensaver show at Stanford last fall and he's doing a portable show that is coming up in New York next year – it's all wireless stuff. He came to us with the idea to create a touring net-art console where we would basically take the shell of a video game and stick a Linux server in it that would have a web-server on it, and serve up certain net-art projects that were adapted to work in an offline environment. Then we would send it around to rural community art centres and inner-city after-school programmes, and places where net-art just doesn't have any presence at all. Places that don't have any tech staff, any systems administrators – maybe even no computers, no Internet connection. The idea is that you basically ship it there, in a refrigerator box, unpack it and just plug it in and it starts up and works. I guess we would send Jim out there to give a talk and generate some interest in it. But there is a lot of concern in the US about this so-called 'digital divide' and the notion that, as interesting as net-art is, access to it is very, very limited and the divide tends to fall along race, class and socio-economic barriers. We're trying to think of ways to bridge those gaps. I find the whole project a little problematic in that we are taking work offline so it limits the kind of work we could include. But I'm hoping that by including artists in the process and by asking them to either make new work or customise their work to function in that condition – it'll probably not even have a keyboard, but maybe just a joystick and a button – that we'll be able to bridge that gap and find a way to get net-art into places where it otherwise has no presence at all.

PETER RIDE:

I'm fascinated by the range of work that you do as an organisation, going from being the intermediary for discussion through to what you've just described now – a very proactive cultural organisation representing work and bringing work to new audiences and identifying what the audiences are. You described various ways in which you locate and provide accessibility to work through your server. Even though you might not be using the conventional gallery approach to curating – selecting a small number of artists – you are still giving people the opportunity to present their work, and in a sense you are the publisher of the work. You will probably find, I guess, that people are doing work for the Rhizome site which might not be located anywhere else. It might be on their own server but you are the main portal to an extended outside world. Where is the line drawn and does it matter whether an organisation like Rhizome describes itself as showing curated work in the way that say, the Dia Center website does? Because you are doing that! As far as your audience is concerned, they'll come to you to see interesting work.

MARK TRIBE:

It is sneaking up on us I think, and it's a little dangerous. We're at the point now where lots of people are coming at us with ideas and partnership opportunities and we don't really have a very clear set of criteria for evaluating opportunities and making decisions about what to do next and how to expand. It's been largely intuitive and it's a debate that goes back and forth between Alex and I. That debate now involves our board which is getting more and more active. Actually, we've just initiated a strategic planning process that will take about six months and we're going to figure out how to expand our mission (if we're going to expand our mission), what kinds of new programmes we should pursue, and how our identity should evolve. When I say 'identity', I don't mean brand, but more like what we're really about – our core vision. But I got a press release the other day – somebody was announcing or re-announcing a new version of a net-art project, and it said that it had been exhibited at ISEA and was included in the Rhizome 'Art-Base' and that just blew me away. That wasn't what it was intended for at all. It's not supposed to be a seal of legitimacy. But clearly the institution has gained a life of its own and so we have to deal with the trappings of that a little bit. I think it's a good question and we're taking some time to really figure out the answer.

I was out at SFMoMA in February to do an event and David Ross and I were talking about this issue – what's the future of Rhizome? He said, 'Well, maybe Rhizome is just a limited time proposition. Maybe it has its relevance for five or ten years then you just stick it somewhere and move on to other things.' Do we want to create a self-perpetuating organism – something that is really sustained; that outlives us in a certain sense so that we can move on and do other things? Rhizome continues to evolve and change and respond to changing times. I think the latter is what we want, but it's problematic because how do you create a sustainable institution without ossifying and becoming bureaucratic and becoming exactly the opposite of what you intended to embody at the start? You see that all the time today with arts organisations that were started between 1968 and 1972 – like The Kitchen, Franklin Furnace and Electronic Arts Intermix, the list goes on and on. Even if they are very clever and are able to evolve and remain relevant, their self-interest ends up becoming a huge priority and they end up doing things for the wrong reasons. So I don't know, it's tough. In a way it was a lot simpler when there was no money and it was a gift economy: it was just a labour of love.

CLAIRE DOHERTY:

I was really interested in what you were saying about filtering. Just to pick up something that we began to talk about this morning: the distinction between the art world, the new media world and the gallery space. I think it seems to me that what you've been talking about is a really interesting model in relation to physical space and whether or not what we could begin to do in terms of galleries is to actually look at programmes that allow for filtering. Essentially what you would end up with are programmes that allow things to come to the surface. So it's far more experimental even if they're within institutions. But I think the other thing that's been coming up in the discussion is this nervousness over actual criteria of judgment. How do we judge them to be significant, whether they be artworks physically within a space or online? I was wondering whether you could talk a little bit about your advisory panel and some of the discussions that you may have had over criteria and judgments?

MARK TRIBE:

Well one thing to note is the advisory panel is not involved in the selection process for the 'Art-Base', although they did help us come up with the selection criteria. Really, what we did was bounce ideas off them more than anything. To be honest, the advisory panel is basically just an e-mail list of twenty people and we send things out to them and then half a dozen will respond at any given time.

The primary two selection criteria for the 'Art-Base' are: is it net-art and is it potentially historically significant? So we define net-art as art that is meant to be experienced online and for which network topology is in some way fundamental or integral. I guess I could imagine somebody doing a bunch of Photoshop art that's never meant to be printed out, it's only meant to be experienced on their website, but that's not net-art. Historical significance is a little bit trickier to determine and fundamentally we put these up as a justification for when we say no, but we almost always – in the case of net-art – say yes. Our goal is to be inclusive, rather than exclusive, and to be as comprehensive as possible. But we look at how aesthetically and conceptually sophisticated the work is as well as how politically relevant it is. We also consider whether or not it's been talked about in places like Nettime, Rhizome or in more mainstream publications. We look at its provenance and whether it was commissioned or exhibited by some interesting place or something like that. But for the most part, if it's net-art then it belongs in there and we accept it.

PETER RIDE:

The commercial model that you outlined is very different from what happens here in the UK because people usually don't make much money selling art. I would say that for most of the people working within the media arts community, ninety-five per cent of their work is funded almost primarily through the public sector or through sponsorship. The notion for most people of a corporate sector or a commercial commodified sector buying work is actually really small.

MARK TRIBE:

Just to clarify, I'm not sure that the percentage is much higher among American media artists. I just think there is that five per cent or so that have found their way into the gallery market. In terms of media art you have Bill Viola and a few others who sell large installations at an institutional level and then sell editions to small individual collectors. That just doesn't exist yet for net-art, but I assume it will. So the question is, how is that going to happen and how can we encourage that to happen in a way that doesn't really do violence to the work? In a way, I think it is just better if the work itself doesn't get sold – or if it does get sold, then it gets sold on an institutional level and not commodified in some way. Maybe it just doesn't get sold at all; maybe a lot of the work ought not to go there, I think.

PETER RIDE:

There was a lot of talk, say five years ago, of there being a hybridity of art production in new media fields, that people were working in commercial fields and in artistic fields, and working to bring them together. But actually, I'd say that we see, within the UK art sector, a polarisation between people who operate in commercial fields doing commercially-driven work and people who are named as new media artists, who often support their practice through very conventional ways – teaching, working within academies. I do look around at the stuff that gets put on artists' websites or filtered sites like yours and it usually comes from people who name themselves up-front as artists working within an artistic context. It doesn't come from people who are simply commercial producers who are doing very interesting work. So just as a specific example, something like the Soda Constructor, by the group Soda, which I think is a brilliant little piece of work and could be shown in all sorts of contexts, doesn't often get shown or talked about in an arts context here. Often people working that way are working with that job pushing the technological solutions, sometimes for very creative purposes. But they don't get taken into an arts discussion. Sometimes the filters work, but sometimes they can actually trap as well.

MARK TRIBE:

It seems like a lot of net-artists in New York have day jobs as designers and programmers. But it is interesting, that liminal zone between artistic and commercial practices. Another example might be the Visual Thesaurus project by Plum, which I think of in many ways as an artwork, but is also a product that they've sold and customised. They're systems innovators – they build things for other people. So this is a commercially-available product. Or 'Netomat' is straddling that line in a really interesting way.

TAMAS BANOVICH:

Half of the works that I was showing first in the 'Can You Digit?' show were by designers and I think there is a serious blur there, because basically all the innovation on the Web, especially at the beginning, came from these people and they considered it their art. So it was an interesting issue in commercial art practice, with art being so-called 'non-commercial', which I think is nonsense because every instance when art enters into any transaction is a commercial transaction, whether it is with the public sector or the private sector. I don't see that big a difference.

SARAH COOK:

I think maybe we should move on and take a break and then let Nina and Karen set up their talk which will bring us back to issues of locality, placement and installations in the real world. Thanks Mark.

[Audience applause]

KAREN GUTHRIE AND NINA POPE*

SARAH COOK:

We have a few issues that came up yesterday that I'm hoping we're still going to get the chance to discuss such as audiences, who benefits, who the work is made for, and how you control the momentum and the velocity – to use Peter Ride's terms – of projects when you launch them out into the world. So to this end, I am pleased to have Nina Pope and Karen Guthrie here to talk about their work.

KAREN GUTHRIE:

Hi. I came up with about three titles for this talk about being commissioned, but they all turned out like 1980s song titles. But I will give you them anyway and you can choose one. The first one was 'They Just Don't Get It'. The second one was 'Tell It Like It Is', and the third one was 'Bite the Hand That Feeds', which is a bit how we

*The full text of this talk has been published by the artists on www.somewhere.org.uk

feel really sitting in front of you, about to say what we're going to say.

We thought the best approach for this talk would be to firstly outline our practice in pragmatic terms and then to describe a few projects from recent years as case studies, tracking them back through the commissioning in terms of the pros and cons, but also being as liberal as possible in hindsight and, as I said, trying not to bite the hand that feeds us – which is a lot of you in this room.

We're finally going to focus on a project called 'TV Swansong', a project that includes our work and seven other new commissions by quite a diverse group of artists. It's our first foray into commissioning and curating a project ourselves. It might sound throughout that we're glossing over details of individual projects, and that is true – we are. But it is in response to the focus of the seminar, which is about curation. So we've got a page of our website up here (somewhere.org.uk). If you want to look at the projects in detail, then that's the place to do it.

For those of you who are here and don't know our work, we've collaborated since 1995 on projects that often combine collaborating with other people with technology or new media. Another recurring theme has been the interface of local and global culture and histories. 'A Hypertext Journal' from 1996 was a live, online trave-logue, and last year we worked with Anna Best and Simon Poulter on 'The Festival of Lying', which was a live event and webcast from Grizedale in Cumbria, based on the Cumbrian pub sport of lying or tall-tale-telling. Other media that we've worked quite a lot in include video, installation and performance.

In our earlier days, such as for 'A Hypertext Journal' in 1995 and 1996, we would often respond to an open commission, fail to get it and carry on with the idea anyway, fundraising and publicising it ourselves. This wasn't really a choice but, like any youngish graduates with no name for themselves, who might show in a warehouse space, this was just our version of doing that – just getting on with it. At this stage, in 1995 and 1996, there were no new media departments at the Arts Council of England or at London Arts Board. In fact, at the time I had a memorable correspondence with the Scottish Arts Council, trying and failing to convince them that one day soon the Internet would be a medium for artists to work in. So we slipped through most of the funding nets that were available at that time, and for 'A Hypertext Journal' we ended up with Peter Ride's personal laptop and a tiny sum from the Photography Department of the Arts Council, and also some money from the The Calouste Gulbenkian Foundation, which has never had new media attached to it, but there's an individual there called Shaneed, who's been an incredibly loyal supporter of ours.

[...]

Our practice at the moment is such that we rarely manage to do more than two projects in one year and we combine that work with on and off income from teaching. We also have a free studio at the moment, which is quite significant, courtesy of Delfina in London. Some of these things aren't specific to a new media practice, but it seems true that we do take on fewer and larger opportunities than most artists. In the last five years we've worked with budgets that go up to about thirty or thirty-five thousand pounds per project. So increasingly the projects that we do do are spanning more than one year and they're being facilitated by a regular team of helpers that we've built up over that time. What Iliyana was saying earlier about networks of friends is really relevant in our case. People like James Stevens of Backspace has probably been the most underpaid but over-helpful member of that group for us for about four years. We probably spend about one or two days a week administering what we do and fundraising for it. These might seem quite trivial things, but I think a lot of people here in the room may not know actually what it is like to be an artist on a daily level. This is what we do really; this is our day job. So it's different perhaps from the American artists that we've been talking about who programme as a day job. We've recently worked increasingly to these commissions and almost exclusively in the UK, which again is not a strategy, but I think it reflects on the long gestation period that our best projects have. That's a difficult thing to sustain abroad, I think, if you're not living in that country. The commissions are spread fairly evenly between the ones that come to us and the ones that we have to apply for. It's quite hard for us to make speculative work because I think you need the space, the technology and the manpower that just isn't available outside the commissioning framework. So more open commissions are coming our way at the moment, and it means that it's less necessary to squash the square peg into the round hole to get through the first stage of a commission brief. But I'll come back to this funding issue a bit later.

From that general outline you can probably guess some of the challenges that are faced by the people that commission us, and perhaps the initial horror for the curator of this work is that it is expensive, in terms of time. That is the case because our work always evolves out of extensive periods of research. When I say research, it sounds like I'm talking about sitting in a library or something, but we've done things like sailed up and down the waterways in Norfolk for weeks on end, or just played online games for weeks on end. So that's what we consider to be research. It's also expensive because there's two of us to pay from a project and lastly, because the media that we use or can use, can be very costly to access and costly to present. By that I mean that a piece might not be suitable for six weeks in a gallery. It might only be destined to be shown once in public. That can also require heavy and extensive marketing to target the right audiences. Of all these costs, you can imagine which one gives first when funds are tight – and they usually are in this area – and it's only recently that we've tried to be really firm about paying ourselves for the time we put into projects. We still do compromise this because at the end of the day, if you want a project to be good then you will give that aspect of it up first, I think.

I think technical issues and expenses also loom quite large on the horizon for smaller arts organisations commissioning this kind of work. They think about something like a webcast as a very daunting thing to have to provide or facilitate and I would say as well that our experiences with the larger organisations like the Tate don't always differ from that.

But, on the plus side for our commissioners – and there are some plus sides – our projects do usually tick this plethora of regional/educational/access/participation/funding priority boxes, and we haven't ever been naïve about that. In fact some of the funding criteria fit our projects so well that you would think that we'd written those guidelines. I think we're more aware about the bottom line 'fundability' of projects than most artists are. I think this is because of the number of self-initiated projects we've done and where we've filled in the application forms and filled in the report form at the end. We don't resent the un-picking of projects to try and fit in with funding criteria and in fact, we actually get quite a lot of satisfaction out of doing that, and linking very left-field ideas into these very carefully constructed, politically-correct priorities. A good example is the 'Festival of Lying', which I mentioned earlier, which was a live event and in a petrol crisis – so it was a small audience – and a webcast as well. In that we managed to embed an educational programme which taught children to lie in an event celebrating Cumbrian culture. So at the end of that I think that everyone was happy: us as the artists, because we were happy to get the RALP (Regional Audiences Lottery

Programme) money via the children and the educational aspect to the project; and the kids because they got to show off doing something that they weren't supposed to do – certainly they weren't meant to be taught to do; and I guess that the Arts Board were happy because they got to tick this fistful of funding priority boxes.

[...]

The other pluses from the commissioning side of practices like ours can include the engagement of the artist outside the gallery and the corresponding debate that we are willing to take on around that, and we are willing to extend that debate very actively within the sort of work that we do. There are other practical advantages, like we can manage ourselves effectively. We can write a press release. We can run a budget meeting. More and more technical challenges are becoming less problematic because of the natural advancement of new media technologies, but also because of these networks of friends, organisations and people developing to be able to carry out things like webcasts, which seem to be fairly mobile. They can move across Britain and set up a webcast from almost anywhere.

So we'll go into some of these points in a little bit more detail later. But I think overall we feel quite fortunate in working with new media – at least in the UK – early on enough to have evolved with the funding strategies that support that practice. So hopefully this is a real dialogue which will continue and it doesn't need to stagnate – the two things, the practice and the funding, can actually keep going in tandem, I hope.

NINA POPE:

I'm going to talk a bit about some work. We're going to start at 1999 with a good patch for us where we were offered Imaginaria / Cap-Gemini funds to bring to fruition a long-term project called 'An Artist's Impression'. We'd also been invited to apply for the Tate Annual Event, which Karen's going to talk about later, which was a one-day commission and part of their pre-opening programme, where they tried to initiate a number of projects before the new building opened.

'An Artist's Impression' is in fact quite a good example of a very mixed bag of funding opportunities and different partners coming in to support it. It began with a very small (five hundred quid) commission from the BBC 2 programme 'The Net', which was open, not just to artists, but to anyone who was going to do something quirky which would provide content for their show. This gave us a chance to do some early research into how people imagined and visualised communities, architectural spaces, and societies on the web, and this led us very specifically to text-based games – MUSHES and MOOs – and other spaces which we came to term as being on the dark underbelly of the Internet.

Later on a slightly larger R&D grant from LAB Digital Initiatives enabled us to continue this research and most of that money was spent being logged onto these games and playing them all day. All of this research eventually led us to wanting to build our own online game and to make a corresponding installation which would, in a way, be a visual metaphor for that space, which was obviously very far from visual. We weren't too specific in our initial funding application but it did serve to secure this R&D funding. At the end of that we then developed a very focussed proposal on how we wanted to take the work forward and how we wanted to write our own game – a MUSH – and how we wanted to relate it both to our earlier works, but also to bring in another thread of research into model railway enthusiasts and the idea that this hobbyist culture could be used as a visual aesthetic to set up a parallel metaphor for the kind of activity we'd encountered on the Internet.

At this point we also got, jointly, a part-time research post at the Southampton Institute for this piece, and it helped us to tick over financially while we were making it. The agreement was that they would get a show and we would give a paper at their conference at the end of it. So it was about eighteen months probably from the beginning of the project to the end, when it was premiered at the ICA (London).

[Slide] This is what happens if you log into the game. I'm not going to try and do it live here. It's a very unsatisfying experience witnessed as a passive member of an audience, but obviously it's fantastic if you log into it directly. As I say, it's text-based. You log in and you arrive in on a small island and you are able to walk around and if other users are logged in then you chat to them in real-time. It's exactly the same technology as every other existing MUSH, of which there are hundreds, if not thousands, on the web. We based the initial descriptions of our game on places which were familiar to us from our memory, so at either end of the island you have a description of, in my case, a small village where I grew up in that seventies dream home. In Karen's case, it's a house on the West coast of Scotland. You probably wouldn't know that if you logged into the game, but we took a decision that we wanted the descriptions to reference something that was very familiar to us, but which had the haze of memory over the top. So we did this mainly to avoid using a lot of the clichéd language that you find in MOOs and MUSHes where it seems that once you open it up to people, they tend to fall back on a very limited number of options to work with, so we just took this on a hunch that it might help the writing that we were doing at the beginning of the game.

[...]

We worked on the game for about six months before the show opened. So the game was up and running and there was quite a good community of players established by the time the show opened at the ICA, and then for a month we were there every day working on the model live. So as people were moving around and changing and building things in the game, in this text-based space, we were attempting to replicate what they were doing on this model in the ICA. In each corner of the room we had workstation areas where we were building stuff.

So this project represents the snowballing of four different funders from different sectors and it wasn't a conscious strategy on our part, but it seemed to work. It showed us that a combination of being opportunistic and optimistic about a project could succeed in moving it forward and also that there was no replacing a very long gestation period for us in order to think about a piece over an extended period for it to succeed in its final outcome. It was interesting to us that the person at the ICA commented that when we bought the model in, they'd got exactly what they were expecting. It was very heartening to us to realise that we'd been able to describe what we were going to do successfully. From the point of view of the funders, we hope that each backed a very specific part of the project so there was no conflict for them. The budget was pretty generous and therefore unproblematic – and most importantly, it was just handed over to us at the beginning and we handled it and we dealt with it independently. The show itself came with a few corporate strings attached, but as we felt in control of the project, this didn't seem or feel too much of an imposition.

Our only real complaint about the ICA show, interestingly, was to do with the PR identity of the show, which was plugged very heavily as digital art. But more than this, I think there was actually a line that said, 'The most interactive art show ever', which obviously we had no say in.

But it meant that everybody walking into the show was expecting to come and click buttons and interact with something, and on being confronted with a large polystyrene island, they were slightly bemused as to what they were supposed to do with that. It meant that they really wanted to use the computers that were our workstations, which we had very deliberately not made open access to the public. This wasn't just a sleight-of-hand on our part, but a deliberate decision because the nature of the online community – in a nutshell – is not something that you can experience in two minutes on a PC in a gallery situation.

[...]

KAREN GUTHRIE:

We're now going to move onto a very different commission process. We're going to talk about 'Broadcast', which was the Tate Annual Event 1999, and in a way it was the flip-side experience of 'An Artist's Impression'. That experience was made more polarised by the fact that we did both projects concurrently towards the end of 1999. Probably a number of you are saying, 'I have never heard of that project, what are they talking about?' and you are certainly not alone. It was one of the worst-marketed things that we'd ever done, and one of those pieces where I forever hear people going, 'that sounds interesting, why didn't I hear about that?' But we're going to get to some of those subjects in a bit.

As we said earlier, it was part of the pre-opening programme that the Tate were doing at the time and Anna Best's 'Wedding Project', when she held a real wedding in Borough Market, was its predecessor. Both of these events took place one day in Borough Market, which was an up-and-coming place at the time and is now a thoroughly gentrified part of South London on the Tate's doorstep.

[Video plays]

To briefly describe the piece, the Borough Market is where Chaucer's Canterbury Tales was sited. We found, through a selection and application procedure, twenty-nine contemporary pilgrims who wanted to make a one-day journey to somewhere significant for them. They chose it. The deal was that they would broadcast us a tale in the market to a live audience, and that tale would be something that we worked on with them and it somehow explained their journey. It was accompanied by a very extensive website that was up before the live event. The day itself was open for people to come in and out of the market for the whole eight-hour period, perhaps catching one or two tales, or perhaps just wandering around this installation which looked very much like an exploded TV set. The day was scheduled in such a way that the pilgrims came in at various specific slots with their live tale, and most of that was designed to accommodate their return journey back to the market, so they actually all returned in person during that day and were interviewed in this TV-style set up. (Nina: They delivered their tale from wherever they'd gone to on their pilgrimage). Somebody went to the South of France and back in one day – that was probably the furthest. I have to say that the mobile phone technology was just fantastically reliable throughout it. It was very easy. There were some projected visuals in the market on the day, but on the whole I would describe it as a radio with pictures. The images were chosen by the pilgrims, and it was really quite a static thing. It was a very audio-led project. You were there really to listen to these voices coming in live and telling you something very intimate about why they had made this journey. I think that was the power of the piece. In this very open, public market, it did look like an intimidating exchange with those pilgrims. But for them, they'd worked with us for many, many months before the actual event. They trusted us and for them, standing where they were with their mobile phone, there was nobody else around, and so I think it was a very intimate exchange for them.

NINA POPE:

[Slide] In the market there was a big screen up so whatever was going out onto the webcast at any time was also going up onto this screen live in the market.

[...]

In preparing for this talk I actually re-read some of the early correspondence that I had with the Tate and I noticed that the commission brief asked us for 'an event with art at its centre', and that is a verbatim quote. This funny emphasis – an event with art at its centre, and not an art event – didn't really strike us as that odd at the time, although I remember thinking about it. In hindsight it should maybe have said something quite significant to us about what they wanted. It's not that we were under any illusions about the aims of the pre-opening programme to gain favour with the local community around the Tate, but we didn't realise how differently they were going to view our project from what went on inside a gallery. Until recently, I guess the Tate was not used to dealing with live artists – it's a collector, an archive. In a nutshell, the experience overall was a bit like working with a dinosaur which had woken up from a very long hibernation. It was a big, impressive organism that somehow didn't really understand what was going on around it. It couldn't keep up to speed. There was a time after this experience, which was very, very tiring, that for us the word 'Tate' was just like a four-letter word.

There were some great things about getting this commission, so I should list them. There was enough money right at the start. We weren't involved in that fund-raising at all and it was really generous. We weren't answerable to anyone except the Tate about the finances, so we were fairly independent. It was also just a very big ego boost to work with a gallery that our mums had heard of for a change. We were flattered! It was a very open brief. Really the market and the one-day event were the two things that we had to bear in mind, but actually we could do more or less what we wanted.

Initially the downside to getting this great-sounding commission involved practical things. Short timescale; it was over the summer, which is a difficult time to work because people are away, and there was a lack of technical expertise in the Tate, or maybe a lack of knowledge about how to tackle those issues. The project was very, very ambitious, but we guessed that that was why we'd been offered the commission and I think we expected the might of the Tate would overcome a lot of those problems. But I have to say that quite soon in the procedure the problems that I think really afflicted the project became quite apparent. I'll just go through some of those, mainly because I think they're very applicable to the way that commissioners generally deal with artists and I think we can all learn something from them.

There were relatively large numbers, we felt, of Tate staff involved in this project and they didn't have specific roles, and their commitments varied quite radically throughout the commissioning procedure. So there was a lack of continuum of individuals and I think meetings, for example, of which there were a great deal in this project, were really affected by that. Meetings with artists in their studios can be quite a lot of fun for arts administrators who don't get out of the office very often. So they came to see us and we gave them a bit of cake from a local cake shop. It was really nice, but for us, it was just another thing stopping us from getting on with the project.

Also, there were certain tasks within the project that, without any logic or discussion even, seemed to be solely the responsibility of the Tate. Whereas there were others that were left for us alone to deal with, and this didn't seem to follow a rationale that we could perceive. Most significantly perhaps, this led us to making a big mistake in the employment of a production company, whose technical skills ended up being worse or way behind ours. But on a smaller scale, it led to us personally negotiating certain things like the seating or the catering for the event with just days to go before it. The problems in communication that this typified were brought to fore on the day of the event. We were presenting, so we had no real ability to interact with the practical aspects of the day once it was actually underway, we just had to be at the fore and present. A really shocking thing happened: a children's workshop appeared at the back of the market and it wasn't directly related to our project. It was about the pre-opening programme and we had not known that it was going to take place, and it did actually cover quite a large area of the market.

NINA POPE:

It had been discussed, but as something that would happen very much to the side of the installation.

KAREN GUTHRIE:

So it seemed to us that, despite specific descriptions about how the market should be installed and how the public experience of the project included not just the content of the tales, but the actual experience of coming into the market and having to negotiate the way the physical space was disorganised, we felt that that had somehow been ignored. It seemed that the Tate felt that they had to add something, quite frankly; that they had to add some interpretation to that experience, and I think the same goes for the foam-board interpretative panels that appeared at that time as well. So that one workshop, for us, was really just icing on the cake about certain communication breakdowns.

Most critical of all I think, was the marketing of this one-off event. Funnily enough, this was the one thing that we thought the Tate would really excel at. But when it came down to it, it seemed to us that the Tate were more concerned with, for example, recruiting celebrity pilgrims, which happily didn't come off. They were more concerned with that than ensuring things like distributing publicity at a really basic street level. A press release, which was totally inaccurate, was released without us actually seeing it. So, these seemingly small cock-ups and missed opportunities, really snowball in significance, I think, for a one-off event.

Needless to say, we worked a lot harder on this than we ever had on a project. We hugely underestimated how tiring it would be to work with twenty-nine people. That's our mistake. And as a result, I guess we felt very personally let down by these problems, because we were so involved with this project and we put ourselves on the line with it so much. The low attendance figures at the event – we'd maybe seen them coming, but we were so snowed under that we felt unable to step in and do something about that. In a way, you could say that that's how it should be: the artist is getting on with doing it, whilst the commissioner is dealing with everything else, but in hindsight we really regret not making more of a fuss when we felt that these things were becoming apparent, and that is our mistake, definitely.

There were some things that Matthew said yesterday about working in the Tate that rang a lot of bells for us actually, although he's a lot more politic than us. It was quite reassuring to hear him talking about trying to change opinions within the Tate and working within that huge, lumbering organism to change ideas of what art actually is with those members of staff – not just how they are treating artists or dealing with a project.

So if anyone's wondering, and you might be, if this is the first time that we've spoken up in such detail about this programme or project, you can rest assured that we did actually submit a feedback report at the end of the commission. Incidentally, that wasn't actually asked for by the Tate, but if there's one thing that commissioners and artists should always do, it is to do that at the end of a project. De-brief and get all that crap out onto the table and discuss where it went wrong – if it went wrong. We did that really quite successfully with the Tate, and it was really instructive. It cleared the air of a lot of these issues.

NINA POPE:

We don't want to end our session on a really downbeat note, so we're going to try and bring together the experiences from 'Broadcast' and 'Artist's Impression' to make a case for this thing that some of you have heard us talk about before – a very specific idea of audience which rejects the Internet as a globally-accessible art form, and instead accepts a more modest, organic idea of interconnected rings of audience affected by our artwork. We've come to realise that this group is a primary audience for us and we, and them, have to be mutually committed to the work for it to function. In effect, this is our most important audience because out of this come other rings of audience, so you have them in the middle, then outside of that you have our friends and acquaintances, or their friends and acquaintances – people who are indirectly involved in the work. Then out from that you might have, at a live event, people who come on the day for example. Then you have people who visit the website while it's actually live. Then you have people who only ever hear about it at a conference or access it through various different types of media. For us, this idea of rings of audience has become very critical.

[...]

KAREN GUTHRIE:

After such a critical discussion you are probably thinking, with justification, if commissioners are so lousy why don't they just get on and do it themselves? Which is exactly what we are doing with 'TV Swansong'.[1] And we're quite happy to be asked about it in two years' time and talk about all the mistakes that we've made throughout it. As we said at the beginning, there are eight new commissions in 'TV Swansong'. The brief was for the artists to respond to a site or situation made significant through television. And specifically television, not film. And we are curating it, rather than contributing a work. The project looks at the current flux in TV culture as convergence media comes on board and the national conversation that was TV viewing in Britain over the last twenty or thirty years comes to an end. I don't think it could be reborn in the same state.

It originated in an idea with Peter Ride of DA2: Nina and he both discussed the possibilities of working with new media in rural places and we had a lot of interest in doing places that were made famous by television, like 'Heartbeat' or 'All Creatures Great and Small' and a lot of the early research we did focused on what was it like for those communities to be made famous by TV. And the people in them – how did it affect them? So the project as a whole is a response, in the way we are controlling it, to the criticisms that we have made. But it is fuelled by a genuinely experimental approach to commissioning artists from a diverse, often not new media, background to work with the tools, approaches and methodologies that we have access to because of our background. And these are things that we consider worthy of a higher profile in general arts practice. We feel that we are enabling a lot of artists that don't have access to that to get on board with some of the best things that have emerged out of new

1. 'TV Swansong' premiered eight new commissions by artists through a live webcast on 20.03.02 (www.swansong.tv).

media practice in the last six or seven years, as we've been involved with it here.

In practical terms we funded a lot of the R&D by doing some pilot projects – and by that I actually mean art projects. That's an interesting way to develop a model for a project, by saying 'here's an art project that describes what this might be like', not 'here's a bit of A4'. And for the first time we've employed a project manager to deal with the day-to-day admin of what we do, because we find it such a complex project, and that is quite a big step.

The key part of this project overall, how we're going to bring together these strands, is that it rejects the retrospective gallery show as access to essentially live or time-based works. Most of the projects are live events which will be filmed in some way, and they are happening in all sorts of different locations, and that's very important. Shows like 'Democracy', which was curated by the Curating Course at the Royal College of Art, is typical of a tendency that we are perceiving which is to collect and present a neat documentation of live and time-based work and to present it as that, rather than promoting access to live work, or better still commissioning it. We're going to launch the project by using a one-day webcast, which will be a window onto them. Some projects will happen on that day and others will be starting or will have finished by the time that day happens. But what they will all have in common is a dual identity, at a local level of where they are taking place live, and also nationally, through the identity of the project and the webcast. So obviously maintaining this dualism is going to be a massive marketing task, so we have, right from the start of the project, tried to integrate that into the fabric of the commissions and the way we've talked about them to people. We hope that really innovative marketing and brand management will be an integral part of the project. There will also be a publication and a conference which will review the project after it happens.

And so what is important about it so far is that it is a practice-led, holistic approach, coming from us as artists. So we've initiated the project with artists meetings for anyone who was considering applying, and we've held them regularly ever since with all the artists together. It is a way of giving them ownership of the project and up till now it seems to be working very well as an approach; the most striking thing is that this very diverse group of artists – some of whom had never seen a webcast, don't send e-mails, that's the kind of group we've got – are responding to it together and generating ideas for marketing and education and how we can kind of get the project out in a very together way. I think that is surprising to us. And they don't feel like tacked-on funding magnets. So that is the artist-led activity of the project, which we hope to maintain throughout it.

Having said all this, it's obvious that we can't achieve a big project like this without good partnerships with existing organisations. We're not an organisation, we're not a company. It's made us wise-up a bit about how to work with partners. So obvious partners would include terrestrial television. But from other projects we've done, TV can be really unreliable and flaky, and so a challenge for 'TV Swansong' is how to work with that frame of reference. Do we do it or just not bother? Getting on TV is not the holy grail of the project, but because it is not a critique of TV it is important to consider how we might relate the project to the space of TV. We've had other ideas we'd really like to go with the project, for example, projects which would allow people to send in digital films and animation. But things like that can only be handled by big organisations with infrastructures to deal with it. So the challenge is how do we retain our ideals and identity of the project independently whilst accessing those major frameworks?

As a way of rounding up this, I want to give some guidelines for how artists and commissioners can work successfully.

The first one I've written is: what is the legacy of new media work? For instance, the archive of 'Broadcast' was finally finished with money from another exhibition that wanted to show that work. In other words, another gallery stood up and said, 'can you finish up that work? Can you make it into a video that we can show and we'll give you the money for it?' And that archive actually ended up back in the 'Broadcast' Tate archive. So in a funny way we didn't complete the archive transaction with the Tate until we were forced to by another organisation. The legacy of that project is, as everyone knows, that the Mongrel and Simon Patterson pieces are known as the first web-commissions at the Tate. On the Website for the Tate there still is no link that I can find to our project. And it is just tiny things like that that help the legacy of the work that you've put into a one-off, live or new media event go on. So I would urge commissioners to think about that. Maybe you end up giving your archive to a gallery or institution and it isn't ideal, but think about how that work can go on and spread out.

The other thing is specific marketing. It is so important to market this sort of work effectively and to keep generating new ideas.

Trust your artists. If you're going to give your artists a really big commission, don't breathe down their necks. Trust them to do something good. And don't get hysterical if they change the brief a few times. That seems really obvious, but that feeling of trust from a commissioner really helps you do something good.

And just as simply, keep a continuum, so that the group of people working with your artists stay on that project and see it through to the end, if possible.

Maybe a more conceptual thing to end on is: where does the art begin and end in one of these new media commissions? If we're talking about imaginary ways of practice and new spaces to make art in, it's really important to establish with your artists where it begins and ends. It might begin with the press release. That might be something that you have to do together, it might not be something that you can just send out and hope that the artist approves of. So just establishing the parameters of where they are actually operating and continually reviewing that to see if you've got it right is really important. Don't make any assumptions about what the artist does and doesn't want to control. And I think that's summing up what we wanted to say. I hope that has been instructive and provides some debate.

[Audience applause]

ILIYANA NEDKOVA:

I'd like to step out of the kitchen of Karen and Nina – thanks for letting us in. What struck me is that very early on, from your early work 'A Hypertext Journal', all the way through to the pilgrimage 'Artist's Impression', is that you seem to be fascinated or obsessed with the journey and the travelogue. I guess there's a bit of a rehabilitation of the idea of cultural tourism here. I do appreciate that, because we tend to shy away from saying, 'yes, we are cultural tourists'. But what strikes me is that you're bringing this additional quality aspect to cultural tourism, which is your excellent way of storytelling. Do you find that this is the way forward – digital storytelling – and is that at the core of the new digital film culture that's emerging? Because apparently the technology will be irrelevant at some point, but the stories and the way that you tell them, and the people that have been involved in them and who have been given a chance to tell their story, is probably much more of the essence.

NINA POPE:

I am going to link it back to something rather prosaic –
unfortunately it is to do with the Tate again – but for me,
the most upsetting point at the interchange with them was
when it became clear that they thought the content of the
event was too boring and that they would have to bring in
something else to supplement that and keep people in the
space. To me personally, it was so upsetting that they
didn't think that the content of these twenty-nine stories
was interesting enough, when to me, there was more
content in those twenty-nine stories than you could see in
a week's TV. That, for me, was the critical point at which I
realised that there was some fundamental breakdown of
our perception of it and their perception of it. Because,
yes, I think there is a great strength in opening up a space
for people to talk about things in that way.

KAREN GUTHRIE:

But a lot of the new technology – not in the art sense, but
more broadly – has been about enabling people to tell
their stories much more easily and to a broader audience.
A lot of what we do taps into the lower range of the
technical register. You know, things like MUSHes and
MOOs and e-mail have always been the most important
parts of our work and they're not the high-end delivery
medium.

[...]

CHRIS BYRNE:

Nina and Karen's presentation raised some questions in
my mind about the roles of artists and curators, but also
specifically their role as curators, facilitators or producers
of other people's work. It's something that I have in
common with them, because I trained as an artist rather
than as a curator or producer. It seems to be a dying

breed of practitioner that turns into a curator. Does that give us any greater insight into the difficulties on the other side of the coin? Should curators be forced to practice as artists?

KAREN GUTHRIE:

But does it happen the other way around?

HANNAH REDLER:

Arguably the project that Nina and Karen did before 'TV Swansong', where they had a curatorial role and even with the project at the ICA – 'An Artist's Impression' – had a curatorial element in that you were convening between an awful lot of people's different visions and realising that vision, even if the project was very clearly yours. But there's a big bleeding edge, particularly within new media, when you've got to work as a team. It's not really an individual process in the way that painting potentially is.

KAREN GUTHRIE:

Yes, but I don't think the blurring of the roles within our projects is happening because of new media. I think it's actually happening because of the way we work and even if we were working sculpturally, those roles would happen. We organise people, but we write our own Web pages. We don't work with a programmer in that aspect, so it's a cottage industry that has us changing lots of hats until we get too big and we can't do that anymore – which is probably now!

[...]

PETER RIDE:

It's very interesting that you haven't actually bracketed yourself as being new media practitioners: as you said,

Karen, you're very interested in emerging forms of work for new spaces. Some of your work uses very old media forms. It's just that these are new ways of operating and they are very complex, they are very messy and sometimes the projects involve a massive number of people with wildly different expectations and sometimes they all come together at one point and sometimes they don't. I dare say that if we had a group of curators here working in other arts areas, particularly from live performance, that sort of distributive complex agenda would appear as a really typical thing.

[...]

NINA POPE:

Apart from 'TV Swansong', we have made a real point of stating from the outset that the pieces are made with us – the intention is very much that we're making them as artists and not as curators or producers. 'Swansong' is definitely out on a limb compared with all the other work in that we are saying, 'okay, we're making our own piece within this, but we are also trying to organise and bring together other artists.' With all our other projects, it's been really important to state all the way through that the whole of that organisational thing is part of our art-making for us and I think that will remain so post 'Swansong'.
Sometimes it's hard for people to understand that, I think. That's not peculiar to new media. I mean Anna Best isn't a new media artist, but she's had similar problems getting people to take on what she's doing as her art practice, and that's something that we have in common.

BERYL GRAHAM:

One of the things I've noticed is that of the number of speakers and participants here today, you all have something to do with research either in a formal or informal way. You mentioned some of the funding coming from the Arts and Humanities Research Board, which would help you to do process-led projects as well as the finished product. It has not really been talked about a huge amount, but it's possibly something which will become more and more common in the future.

SELECTED CONCLUDING REMARKS
(Inspired by and following on from Nina Pope and Karen Guthrie's presentation)

MATTHEW GANSALLO:

I just wanted to say that these institutions that are now stepping into the perimeter and looking at Web art – we have to understand that this is a new area for them and the complicated process of explaining Net art to curators who have managed a collection for years is to be expected. It is not necessarily a bad thing; it is what we have to learn from now, and this will encourage so much more writing and so much more debate and conferences like this in order to lessen fears. Even when I began to work with Internet and Web art and art on the Net, there was a huge amount of confusion about it – about how to do it, about the community of it, about what was going on – because they didn't know anything about it. So even though I feel I have crossed over, I can sympathise with curators. When you are working on a Website and and an artist says, 'I'm going to do this and do that', you have to question if it is going to impact on what you are doing, in terms of marketing and press and so on. So I hope that we have all learnt from the stories that have come through and I hope that is something that we can pick up on when we are working with institutions who must be commended for saying, 'we want to find out more. We might not know what we are doing, but please guide us to this first step.'

[...]

CLAIRE DOHERTY:

I think the important thing to recognise is there are different types of curatorial models. Perhaps what we're saying is because a lot of this work is new – we're talking about something maybe fifteen years old – there are new parameters, new systems of distribution, new ways to handle it curatorially. Those are some of the things that haven't filtered down. Just to reply to what people have been saying about whether or not there's some way in which this information could be shared, the Arts Council, through their Curatorial and Professional Development Scheme, wanted to produce a series of annual publications online and in print, which would include a series of case studies. The idea behind this was to try and disseminate all these experiences and skills to have new strategies and new types of models, especially for those young curators in local authority museums and who therefore don't have the resources to come to conferences like this, and also to artists who are coming up through art school.

MARIA STUKOFF:

Perhaps also to older curators too, who don't have access or who don't actually want to go and touch the stuff.

CLAIRE DOHERTY:

Absolutely. Try and communicate some of those ways of dealing with projects that don't necessarily have outcomes, to find outcomes or exit strategies.

KAREN GUTHRIE:

Yes, I think it's so important that the feedback from these experiences gets disseminated. I think it is transferable to so many different experiences and it stops us feeling so much like wingers if we feel it has an outcome! [Laughter]

PETER RIDE:

I do think that there needs to be ways to disseminate information. Forums like this are fantastic because they create rapport and people remember stuff. But it's also about getting information from sector to sector. Some kind of forum which is about hanging dirty linen out publicly without being embarrassed would be good, because I think what Nina and Karen have done is very brave and there are people here who, at various times, have found it hard to be public about the problems that they've encountered because there are reputations and professional implications, and there aren't very many safe amnesty zones in which you can do it. I think it would be incredibly useful if those were facilitated because there could be a lot of learning in advance from where other people have had run-ins; it would be really useful for anticipating things that can happen in the future.

KAREN GUTHRIE:

Sarah, this is a chance for you to plug CRUMB as a place where these things can be formalised.

PAMELA WELLS:

I think there is a reason why new media artists and digital media practitioners are here together – because as an artist, the messier you work, the more ephemeral the performance, the more you need to work with new media and also the more you need to work together. So you do need to question the existing curatorial models and you need to say, 'why is it we're doing this?' and 'how are we doing it?' and as artists and curators, to collaborate to question those models.

SMALL RADIUS CINEMA PROGRAMME 8
b.small radius
May 10–01
presents ...

SENTIENT MOMENTS from an array of animal, vegetable and mechanical entities

STARRING sinister air planes, undercover sheep, heroic eggplant & emotional toys.

The running order:

Hocus Focus – Sam Easterton 1999 [USA] 5 mins
A video camera is brought to a fortune teller for its own crystal ball reading.

No Sunshine – Bjorn Melhus 1997 [Germany] 6 mins
Twin humanoids float in space, burbling fragments of early Stevie Wonder songs.

Bit Plane – Bureau of Inverse Technology 2000 [USA]
14 mins
A tiny BIT spy plane infiltrates the glittering heart of the Silicon Valley, California.

[interval]

World of Survival – Phil Patiris 1996 [USA] 1 min
Animal kingdom thriller.

The People Shop – Pablo Leighton 1998 [USA] 5 mins
Edited revolutionaries.

Organismes – Chris Dooks 2000 [USA] 2 mins

Squid vid.

The Anatomical Theater of Peter the Great – Rachel Mayeri 1999 [USA] 12 mins
A genetic anomaly: 100 Peter the Greats and 100 Catherines attend dinner.

[interval]

A Sheep in Wolf's Clothing – Sam Easterton 1999 [USA] 5 mins
A sheep is outfitted with a helmet-mounted video camera and VCR backpack.

Fluffy Tamagotchi – Paul Granjon 1998 [UK] 2 mins
How to build your own friend [from the Big M touring video programme].

Kung Fu Kitchen – Jeff Warmouth 2000 [USA] Quicktime, 5 mins
Violent vegetable scenario.

small radius cinema programmed by Kate Rich. Thanks to Sneha Solanki, Sarah Cook, Beryl Graham, BALTIC, Michelle Hirschhorn, Craig Baldwin/Other Cinema, Lux Distribution, ISIS ARTS & the Big M video programme.

SPEAKERS' BIOGRAPHIES

TAMAS BANOVICH

Tamas Banovich is the co-founder and co-director of Postmasters Gallery, New York (first opened in East Village in December 1984, moved to Soho in 1989, relocated again to Chelsea in September 1998). While showing artists working in all media, Postmasters is committed to art made with new technologies (digital and multimedia works). Their now seminal exhibition 'Can you Digit?' showed digital projects on 30 computer stations in March 1996, and was followed a year and a half later by 'MacClassics (the immaculate machines)'. Recent exhibitions include 'Behind the Firewall' and exhibitions of the work of Vinyl Video, Sawad Brooks and Beth Stryer, and etoy.

SARAH COOK

Sarah Cook is a doctoral research student at the University of Sunderland in conjunction with BALTIC, the Centre for Contemporary Art, investigating the practice of new media curating. She has worked in a curatorial capacity at the Banff Centre for the Arts (Canada), the Walker Art Center (Minneapolis, USA), and the National Gallery of Canada (Ottawa). When not online working on CRUMB she is a project coordinator at Locus+.

VUK COSIC

Vuk Cosic is a retired net.artist based in Ljubljana. Since retiring (in 1996) he has created new pieces for Videopositive 2000 in Liverpool ('ASCII Architecture') and 'A History of the Future' at BALTIC (www.thisistherealmatrix.com). He was chosen as the Slovenian Representative at the 2001 Venice Biennale where, as part of his project 'Net.Art Per Me' he curated an exhibition of net.art titled

'Temporary Autonomous Pavilion'. He was one of the founders of Ljudmila – a digital media lab for artists in Slovenia and co-founder of the ASCII Art Ensemble.

MATTHEW GANSALLO

Matthew Gansallo was a senior research fellow at the Tate Gallery's National Programme when he was invited to commission works for Tate-Website. He is an international curator and has studied art and architecture. He assisted on the Lagos section of Tate Modern's exhibition 'Century City' (2001) and is currently an education consultant for Tate Britain.

BERYL GRAHAM

Beryl Graham is a post-doctoral research fellow at the University of Sunderland and an artist. She is the co-editor and founder of the AHRB-funded project CRUMB: the Curatorial Resource for Upstart Media Bliss. She is at the forefront of developing learning materials for postgraduate art-practice-led research. Her doctoral research was a study of audience relationships with interactive computer-based visual artworks in gallery settings. She has made low-tech games in Moscow, Seattle, and Bangalore.

KAREN GUTHRIE AND NINA POPE

Karen Guthrie and Nina Pope have collaborated since 1995 on diverse art projects using new technologies ranging from video to performance to broadcasting. Their piece 'A Hypertext Journal' (1996), was a live online trave-logue following Boswell and Johnson's 'Journey to the Western Isles'. Having recently completed residencies at Grizedale (with subsequent exhibitions of those projects at Collective Gallery in Edinburgh and Q Arts in Derby), they are now organising 'TV Swansong' – eight new commissions based on sites or situations that have been 'made famous' via television.

ILIYANA NEDKOVA

Presently working with New Media Scotland, Edinburgh, as a curator-in-residence, Iliyana Nedkova is a producer and researcher of old and new media art events. Since 1995 Iliyana has been an Associate Curator with the Foundation for Art and Creative Technology (FACT), Liverpool, and more recently a PhD candidate exploring Curatorial Theory and Practice of Digital Art at the Liverpool John Moores University. Iliyana regularly delivers talks at various contemporary art fora and publishes both in her native Bulgaria and abroad. Recent curatorial projects and publications include Desktop Icons (www.mediascot.org); Blind Dating Technology (www.blinddata.net) and Crossing Over (www.crossingover.org) – an annual Micro-festival of Digital Film Culture co-produced with Nina Czegledy.

JULIAN STALLABRASS

Julian Stallabrass curated the exhibition 'Art and Money Online' at Tate Britain which included works by Lise Autogena and Joshua Portway, Redundant Technology Initiative and Jon Thomson and Alison Craighead. In addition to being a writer and photographer he is the author of 'High Art Lite' and 'Gargantua: Manufactured Mass Culture'. Stallabrass is also a lecturer at the Courtauld Institute of Art in London. His book 'Internet Art: The Online Clash of Culture and Commerce' will be published by the Tate in 2002.

THOMSON & CRAIGHEAD

Jon Thomson and Alison Craighead are prolific media artists developing installations for galleries, specific sites, and since 1996, the web. Working with new technology for nearly ten years, Thomson & Craighead have shown in 'Art and Money Online' at Tate Britain ('CNN Interactive just got more interactive'), with Film and Video Umbrella ('Slipstream') and at SFMoMA in the exhibition '010101' ('E-poltergeist'). Thomson lectures at the Slade School of Fine Art in London. Craighead is currently a researcher at the University of Westminster.

MARK TRIBE

Mark Tribe is an artist and an entrepreneur who founded Rhizome.org. Rhizome is an online community space for people who are interested in new media art. Rhizome's activities focus on presenting artworks by new media artists, critics and curators, fostering critical dialogue and preserving new media art for the future. In 2001 Mark curated an exhibition at Moving Image Gallery in New York of Net-art ephemera.

PARTICIPANTS

Karen Alexander, British Film Institute
Eddie Berg, Foundation for Art and Creative Technology
Sharon Bailey, Isis
Jon Bewley, Locus+
Susanne Bieber, Tate Modern
Thora Johansen, Bifrons Foundation
Rob Bowman, MoMA Oxford
Reuben Braithwaite, artist
Steven Bode, Film and Video Umbrella
Jenny Brownrigg, artist
Chris Byrne, New Media Scotland
Joanna Buick, Arts Council of England
David Butler, Globe Gallery
Helen Cadwallader, New Media officer, Arts Council of England
Veronique Chance, artist
Clemeni Christoforu, Isis
Mathieu Copeland, artist
Nina Czegledy, ISEA
Mark Daniels, Northern Architecture
Claire Doherty, Spike Island
Debbie Fenwick
Bronac Ferran, Collaborative Arts, Arts Council of England
Claire Fitzsimmons, Tate Modern
Portland Green
Jeanine Griffin, Site Gallery
Dew Harrison, University of West England
Gill Haworth, Watershed
Tony Harrington, Forge
Lorna Healy, Tate Britain
Patrick Henry, Museum of Photography, Film and Television
Deanna Herst, Axis
Susanah Hewlitt, artist

Michelle Hirschhorn
James Hutchinson, artist
Shona Illingworth, artist
Clive Jackson, artist
Pauline Johnson, Northern Gallery for Contemporary Art
Judith King, English Heritage
Wendy Kirkup, artist
Joasia Krysa, Senior Lecturer in Interactive Media,
MediaLab Arts, University of Plymouth, Curator Caiia-Star
Wendy Law, Scottish Arts Council
Jem Legh, Arts Council of England
Francis McKee, CCA Glasgow
Fin McMorran, artist
Terry Mee, Newcastle College
Maria Moreira, artist
Nat Muller, V2
Taylor Nutall, Folly
Danielle Olsen, Wellcome Trust
Lauren Parker, Victoria and Albert Museum
Anna Pepperall, Gateshead Libraries and Arts
Shaun Perkins, artist
Kathy Rae Huffman, Hull Time Based Arts
Hannah Redler, C/Plex
Vivienne Reiss, Arts Council of England
Peter Ride, DA2
Monica Ross, artist
Paul Scott, University of Newcastle
Mariam Sharp, Arts Council of England
Dominic Smith, Laing Art Gallery
Helen Smith, Waygood Gallery
Philip Smith, Southern Arts
Sneha Solanki, artist
Louise Sorensen
Jem Southern, artist
John Stevens, Faculty of Medicine, University of
Newcastle
Heather Stewart, British Film Institute

Calum Stirling, artist
Paul Stone, Visual Arts North East
Maria Stukoff, artist, IDEA
Adam Sutherland, Grizedale
Helena Swatton, artist
Adinda van t'Klooster, artist
Alessandro Vincentelli, Northern Arts
Mark Waugh, Live Art, Arts Council of England
Pamela Wells, Wallsall Youth Arts
Tony White, Arts Council of England
Amber Wykes, artist, Norwich Arts Centre

URLs

VUK COSIC

www.ljudmila.org/~vuk
www.thisistherealmatrix.com
www.labiennialdivenezia.net

BERYL GRAHAM:

www.newmedia.sunderland.ac.uk/crumb

JULIAN STALLABRASS:

www.tate.org.uk

TAMAS BANOVICH

www.postmastersart.com/

MATTHEW GANSALLO:

www.tate.org.uk

ILIYANA NEDKOVA:

www.crossingover.org
www.virtualrevolutions.net
www.blinddata.net

THOMSON&CRAIGHEAD:

www.thomson-craighead.net
www.slipstream.uk.net

MARK TRIBE:

www.rhizome.org
www.movingimagegallery.com

KAREN GUTHRIE AND NINA POPE:

www.somewhere.org.uk
www.tvswansong.tv

OTHER UK NEW MEDIA ARTS ORGANISATIONS:

www.da2.org.uk
www.fvu.co.uk
www.mediascot.org
www.locusplus.org.uk
www.fact.co.uk
www.peer2peer.org.uk
www.irational.org
www.lovebytes.org.uk
www.channel.org.uk
www.iniva.org
www.metamute.com
www.timebase.org
www.watershed.co.uk
www.test.org.uk

SITES PERTAINING TO OTHER SEMINAR ATTENDEES:

www.v2.nl
www.moma.co.uk
www.artscouncil.org.uk
www.north.org.uk
www.uwe.ac.uk
www.nmsi.ac.uk
www.scottisharts.org.uk
www.wellcome.ac.uk
www.dundee.ac.uk
www.c-plex.co.uk
www.southernarts.co.uk
www.grizedale.org.uk
www.repro.org.uk
www.artsonline.com
www.njn.net/starts

www.fmcc.org.uk/medialab
www.axisvm.nl
www.digibodies.org
www.isea.qc.ca
www.sarai.net

OTHER USEFUL / MENTIONED SITES:

www.arts.org.uk
www.sfmoma.org
010101.SFMoMA.org
www.walkerart.org
aen.walkerart.org
www.mnk.zkm.de
www.thing.net
www.mecad.org
www.isea.qc.ca
www.verybusy.org
www.easylife.org
www.artsconnected.org/millennialmuseum
www.whitney.org/datadynamics
www.whitney.org/bitstreams
www.banffcentre.ab.ca
www.diacenter.org
www.anat.org
www.c3.hu